Metal Clay AND Mixed Media Jewelry

Metal Clay AND
Mixed Media Jewelry

Innovative Projects Featuring Resin, Polymer Clay, Glass,
Fiber, Concrete, Collage Materials, and More

SHERRI HAAB

WATSON-GUPTILL PUBLICATIONS/NEW YORK

When using kilns and other firing devices and methods, readers are strongly cautioned to follow manufacturers' instructions and warnings. If you are pregnant or have any known or suspected allergies, you may want to consult a doctor about possible adverse reactions before using any suggested products or performing any procedures outlined in this book. The techniques and materials described in this book are not intended for children.

First published in 2007 by Watson-Guptill Publications, Nielsen Business Media, a division of The Nielsen Company
770 Broadway, New York, NY 10003
www.watsonguptill.com

All photography by Dan Haab, unless otherwise noted.

Library of Congress Cataloging-in-Publication Data

Haab, Sherri.
    Metal clay and mixed media jewelry : innovative projects featuring resin, polymer clay, glass, fiber, concrete, collage materials, and more / Sherri Haab.
        p. cm.
    ISBN-13: 978-0-8230-3062-0 (alk. paper)
    ISBN-10: 0-8230-3062-8 (alk. paper)
  1. Jewelry making. 2. Precious metal clay. I. Title.
    TT212.H37 2007
    745.594'2—dc22
                        2006014182

Senior Acquisitions Editor: Joy Aquilino
Editor: Michelle Bredeson
Art Director: Julie Duquet
Designer: Areta Buk/Thumb Print
Senior Production Manager: Alyn Evans

Manufactured in Malaysia

First printing, 2007

2 3 4 5 6 7 8 9 / 15 14 13 12 11 10 09 08 07

ACKNOWLEDGMENTS

Thank you to Robert, Celie, Michelle, Cassy, Wendy, and Lora for the great projects.

To all of the artists who assisted with the projects and gallery pieces, thank you.

Special thanks to Joe, Speedy, and Eric at PMC Supply for your support and technical help with the projects.

Thank you to all of the manufacturers who supplied products and support.

And thank you to Dan, Michelle, David, and my friend Jacqueline for help with photography.

This book was made possible in part through support from the PMC Guild.

Contents

Using Metal Clay as a Support or Bezel   70

Color, Images & Surface Design   108

METAL CLAY is an exciting material unlike any other. It is a soft, nontoxic clay that consists of microscopic particles of precious metal suspended in a mix of organic binder and water. Under a microscope, the metal particles look like tiny round spheres (imagine gumballs in a machine), with binder filling the spaces in between. Metal clay is smooth and pliable and can be manipulated like any other type of clay, such as ceramic, porcelain, or modeling clay. Metal clay can be stamped, textured, rolled, and shaped into jewelry, beads, and small sculptural pieces. After the clay has been sculpted, it is left to dry and fired in a kiln or by torch. When metal clay is fired, the binder burns away, and the metal particles fuse together, creating a piece that is fine silver (.999) or 22- to 24-karat gold. The metal can then be finished with a variety of techniques traditionally used by jewelers and metalsmiths to produce stunning pieces of silver and gold jewelry.

Metal clay was developed in Japan in the early 1990s, and since its introduction in the United States, there has much enthusiasm for this material in the jewelry craft world. Artists

LEFT: FUNNY FAIRY
by Susan Gifford Knopp
This delightful pendant was created by applying cloisonné enamel to PMC and embellishing it with cubic zirconia stones.

BELOW: IMAGE TRANSFER BRACELET
by Sherri Haab
Applying collage images to fired metal clay produces a miniature work of wearable art. This bracelet is a variation on the project on page 123.

OPPOSITE: BEADS
by Kelly Russell
Kelly combined metal clay with polymer clay to create these unique pieces reminiscent of antiquities. (Photo by Robert Diamante.)

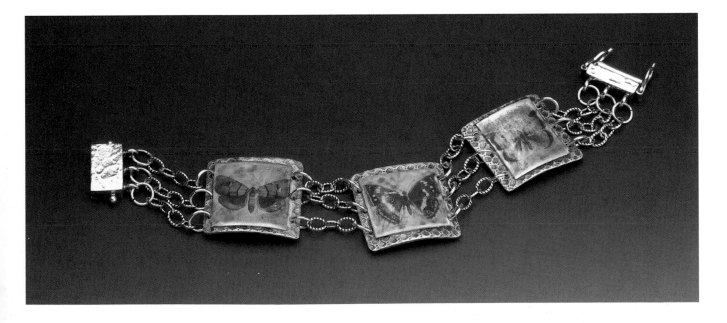

from jewelry backgrounds, as well as from other disciplines, have developed many techniques for incorporating metal clay into their work, and there are now online message groups, magazine articles, and juried events showcasing the wonders of metal clay.

One direction that the art of metal clay was destined to take was that of mixed media. Now that more and more artists are familiar with metal clay, it is being combined with many different materials. Glass enamels, glass cabochons, ceramics, and some colorful stones can be fired with metal clay. Metal clay also provides a new direction for incorporating popular art materials such as polymer clay, resin, collage papers, fiber, paints, and concrete into jewelry. Lots of texture and color are being added to metal, resulting in pieces that push the limits of what silver and gold jewelry can be. The ability to hand-sculpt silver and then choose a variety of media to complement the silver is very exciting. This book explores new ideas and techniques for combining metal clay and other materials and features gallery images of mixed media pieces by talented artists to inspire you along the way.

ABOVE: WOLF PIN *by Pattie Leota Genack*
In this unusual design, a carved tagua nut is framed by PMC accented with enamel.

RIGHT: BARNACLE BRACELET *by Wendy Wallin Malinow*
This organic-looking cuff is formed from PMC3 encrusted with gems. (Photo by Courtney Frisse.)

OPPOSITE: BUTTERFLIES NECTAR *by Kelly Russell*
A perfume amphora sculpted from metal clay forms the centerpiece of this stunning necklace. (Photo by Robert Diamante.)

Metal Clay Essentials

I f you've never worked with metal clay, you'll find everything you need to know to get started in this chapter: an overview of the different types of metal clay on the market, the basic tools and supplies, and essential techniques used to create metal clay jewelry. For those who are already familiar with this exciting medium, this chapter provides a refresher course or a handy reference.

Types of Metal Clay

THERE ARE TWO BRANDS of metal clay on the market: Precious Metal Clay® (PMC) and Art Clay® Silver. Both brands come in several varieties, as well as slip (or paste), syringe, and paper forms, and new types of metal clays and products continue to be developed. Each type of metal clay has distinctive qualities that make one preferable to another for a specific application. The particular project you are making or technique you are employing, as well as your artistic style, will dictate which clay to use.

PMC PRODUCTS

Precious Metal Clay was developed in Japan in 1991 by the Mitsubishi Materials Corporation and first introduced in the U.S. in 1996. Mitsubishi continues to produce new PMC products. The PMC Guild (www.pmcguild.com) offers a newsletter, conferences, workshops, and certification programs to learn more about PMC.

PMC STANDARD PMC Standard, or original PMC, was the first metal clay developed. It consists of flake-shaped particles that allow more binder to fit in between them, resulting in smooth clay with excellent workability. Because it contains more binder than any of the other formulas, it shrinks more in the firing process (25–30 percent) and is great to use for small projects, including charms, and finely detailed pieces. This type of clay is also more porous and less dense in its finished state than other types of metal clay and, therefore, is not as strong. PMC Standard is not recommended for rings, clasps, or other pieces that will endure a lot of stress.

PMC+ This clay is a great all-purpose choice for most projects. It is a bit stiffer than PMC Standard because it contains less binder, but when kneaded and kept moist it works similarly. Its silver particles are denser, and the final fired product is stronger than PMC

Precious Metal Clay comes in several different formulations, including PMC Standard, PMC3, PMC+, paste, syringe clay, and sheet type, all shown here.

Standard. Because of the increased density, it also shrinks less. This type of clay can be fired at several different temperatures and for shorter lengths of time. Certain stones and cork clay, which require lower firing temperatures, can be successfully fired with PMC+.

PMC3 PMC3 clay produces a strong finished product. The clay has smaller, more refined particle shapes and less binder than the other types and is therefore denser. PMC3 can be fired at lower temperatures than PMC Standard and PMC+. It can be fired with enamel, glass, or cork clay, and its lowest firing temperature of 1200°F offers some exciting possibilities. There are a few gemstones that would not survive the firing temperatures required for other metal clay types but will hold up when fired with this clay. Dichroic glass and ceramic pieces can be embedded or surrounded with PMC3 and fired in place without the fear of them breaking or melting. You can also include sterling silver findings that would become brittle if fired at higher temperatures.

Perhaps the most exciting aspect of PMC3 is that you can fire the clay with small, inexpensive handheld torches or portable devices. This is great for workshops where you need portability or do not have access to a kiln.

PMC+ AND PMC3 PASTE Premixed paste, or slip, can be used to "glue" pieces of PMC together, to fill in joints, or to create textures on the surface of a piece. Each type of paste can be used with the corresponding type of clay.

PMC+ AND PMC3 SYRINGE CLAY This product is a softened clay that comes in a ready-to-use syringe. You can use syringe clay to make strong attachments between clay elements. It can also be used to fill in grooves or cracks or to produce lines or ropes

of clay as decorative elements. After opening, keep the uncapped syringe submerged in water. It will remain fresh and ready to use as long as it is not allowed to dry out.

PMC+ SHEET This product is a paper-thin sheet of clay. It dries very slowly and stays flexible while you are working with it. You can fold it, cut it with scissors, or punch it out with paper punches. You can also weave or braid thin strips of PMC+ Sheet, and layers of paper can be laminated using water to make thicker sheets of clay. PMC+ Sheet comes in two sizes: 3 by 12 cm and 6 by 6 cm.

PMC GOLD Gold clay is an alloy of 91.7 percent gold and 8.3 percent silver. The fired clay is 22-karat gold and has a rich yellow color. This clay fires at similar temperatures as silver PMC, which allows you to fire them together. The current PMC Gold has been reformulated from the original version, which required higher temperatures to fire. It also shrinks less than the previous version.

FACE PENDANT #1 *by Wendy Wallin Malinow* This colorful pendant made from PMC+ and polymer clay is representative of Wendy's whimsical style. (Photo by Courtney Frisse.)

Strength After Firing

PMC STANDARD

PMC provides this chart to compare the varying strengths of PMC Standard with PMC+ and PMC3. Notice that PMC+ and PMC3 allow lower firing temperatures.

- ☐ weak
- ▨ pretty good
- ▩ very good

		FIRING TEMPERATURE								
	°F	930	1020	1110	1200	1290	1380	1470	1560	1650
	°C	500	550	600	650	700	750	800	850	900
MINUTES	5									
	10									
	20									
	30									
	60									pretty good
	120									pretty good

PMC+

		FIRING TEMPERATURE								
	°F	930	1020	1110	1200	1290	1380	1470	1560	1650
	°C	500	550	600	650	700	750	800	850	900
MINUTES	5								pretty good	pretty good
	10						pretty good	pretty good	pretty good	pretty good
	20						pretty good	pretty good	pretty good	pretty good
	30					pretty good	pretty good	pretty good	pretty good	pretty good
	60				pretty good	pretty good	pretty good	pretty good	pretty good	pretty good
	120				pretty good	pretty good	pretty good	pretty good	pretty good	pretty good

PMC3

		FIRING TEMPERATURE								
	°F	930	1020	1110	1200	1290	1380	1470	1560	1650
	°C	500	550	600	650	700	750	800	850	900
MINUTES	5	weak	pretty good	pretty good	pretty good	pretty good	pretty good	very good	very good	very good
	10	pretty good	pretty good	pretty good	very good	very good	very good	very good	very good	very good
	20	pretty good	pretty good	pretty good	very good	very good	very good	very good	very good	very good
	30	pretty good	pretty good	pretty good	very good	very good	very good	very good	very good	very good
	60	pretty good	pretty good	pretty good	very good	very good	very good	very good	very good	very good
	120	pretty good	pretty good	pretty good	very good	very good	very good	very good	very good	very good

ART CLAY SILVER PRODUCTS

Art Clay Silver is produced by Aida Chemical Industries, a Japanese company that recycles metals. Art Clay Silver products are similar to PMC products. Art Clay Silver offers many choices of clay for specific projects, as well as accompanying products and tools. All of the Art Clay Silver clays can be fired at a lower temperature or fired with a torch. They are dense and therefore very strong. Art Clay Silver is distributed in the United States by Art Clay World, which offers workshops and certification programs.

ART CLAY SILVER STANDARD This is an all-purpose metal clay. It can be fired at several temperatures, including lower firing temperatures that allow it to be used in conjunction with certain stones, glass, and cork clay.

ART CLAY SILVER SLOW DRY Slow Dry clay contains a binder that makes the clay dry slowly. This allows the artist more working time. Slower drying is handy for those who live in dry climates and for time-consuming techniques such as making rings, braids, or fine ropes. There are a couple of things to keep in mind when working with Art Clay Silver Slow Dry clay: The clay must be allowed to dry thoroughly before firing, and scraps should not be mixed with other types of clay.

ART CLAY SILVER 650/1200 LOW FIRE This is the lowest firing clay of the Art Clay Silver types. It can be fired at low enough temperatures to embed sterling silver findings into the clay, and it can be fired with dichroic glass cabochons, ceramics, and some natural stones. This clay also shrinks less than other types of Art Clay Silver.

ART CLAY SILVER 650/1200 LOW FIRE PASTE Use this paste to attach pieces of unfired clay, to fill in cracks, or to create textures. This product can be used when slip is required for a project.

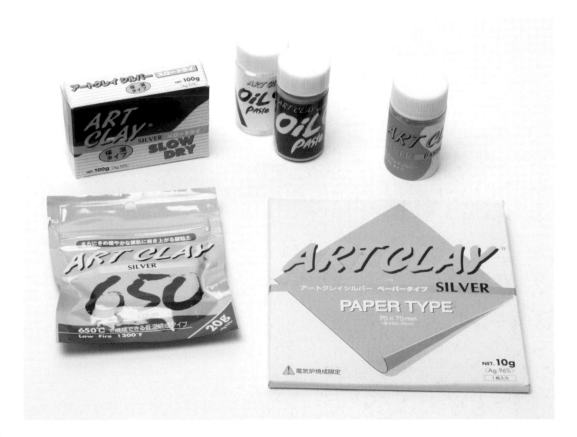

Art Clay Silver products are similar to PMC clays and also come in a variety of formulations.

ART CLAY SILVER 650/1200 LOW FIRE OVERLAY PASTE   This paste is specially formulated for use on glazed porcelain or ceramics and can also be applied on glass. It can be painted on in thin layers as a decorative element and fired. You can also use the paste like slip to join unfired pieces.

ART CLAY SILVER 650/1200 LOW FIRE SYRINGE   This clay is a soft formula that is packaged in a ready-to-use syringe. You can use it to make fine lines of clay, surround stones, or fill in cracks.

ART CLAY SILVER OIL PASTE   Oil Paste is formulated to stick to metal. Use it to attach fired pieces, to make repairs to fired pieces, or to fill in cracks. Fire at 1472°F when refiring pieces repaired with Oil Paste. This product can be used to repair any type of metal clay.

ART CLAY SILVER PAPER TYPE   Paper Type is thin and flexible. It comes in 3- by 3-inch sheets that can be cut, punched, or folded. You can also layer it to make thicker sheets, using water or thin slip to adhere.

ART CLAY GOLD   Sculpt and mold Art Clay Gold as you would silver metal clay. Art Clay Gold fires at a higher temperature (1813°F for 60 minutes). The fired metal is 22-karat gold.

ART CLAY GOLD PASTE   This is a liquid formula of gold that can be applied to silver or painted on glass or porcelain. It comes with a medium that can be used to thin the product down to a glaze consistency.

Which Type of Clay Should You Use?

The projects in this book each suggest that a certain type of clay be used. Factors such as shrinkage rate, firing temperature, strength, and smoothness of the clay were taken into account when choosing the type of clay used. In most cases, the differences between types of clay are very slight, and you can make substitutions for most projects. Just make sure the firing temperatures and working methods will be compatible for the type of clay you decide to use. As you work with metal clay, you may come to prefer one type or brand over another.

MAKING JEWELRY with metal clay requires very little space and just a few simple tools. You can set up at your kitchen table or in a small studio space. Keep the area neat and clean as you work and your tools and supplies close at hand. The best part about using metal clay is that the tools are easy to obtain, and, if you already work with crafts, you may own many tools that can be used with metal clay. You may also be able to substitute tools you already have for some of the suggested tools.

The materials list for each project in the book includes "basic metal clay supplies." These are the common items, described below, which are needed for working with metal clay. I keep them together in a box so they are ready and available to work on a project. This way, I need to gather only the specialty or extra items required for a specific project and I'm ready to get started. Look around and add your own favorites to the basic list below:

WORKING SURFACE Styrene sheets, PVC sheets, plastic mats, laminate countertop surfaces, or Teflon sheets are good surfaces for working with metal clay. Don't panic if the clay sticks to the work surface. Leave the clay item in place, and, as it dries, it will release from the surface. Certain metal surfaces, such as aluminum, react with metal clay, causing the finished pieces to warp and discolor. Do not place metal clay on aluminum foil or aluminum cookie sheets, and avoid other tools with aluminum as well, although minimal contact with aluminum, such as cutting the clay with a cookie cutter, may not affect the silver.

The basic tools and supplies needed to work with metal clay include many common household items such as olive oil, playing cards, and a spray bottle, as well as a few simple craft and ceramic tools.

OLIVE OIL OR BADGER BALM® Keep a small dish of olive oil or a solid ointment called Badger Balm close at hand. Apply a thin film of oil or balm to your hands, tools, and work surface to keep the clay from sticking and drying out. Reapply oil as the clay starts to collect on your fingers. Olive oil or balm can also be used as a mold release. Because they are made from organic ingredients, olive oil and Badger Balm produce less smoke than other types of oils during the firing process. Olive oil is also available in a spray, which can be used on large areas such as plastic texture sheets or large rubber stamps.

WATER AND SPRAY BOTTLE Keep the surface of the clay moist by sprinkling it with water or misting it with water from a spray bottle. Dip a paintbrush or your fingers into the water to join seams or to attach pieces of fresh clay as you work. You can prevent mold growth when storing opened clay that has had water mixed into it by adding a few drops of vinegar to the water. You may want to use distilled water as it has fewer impurities than tap water.

ROLLER A PVC tube or acrylic rod can be used to roll sheets of clay. PVC tubing is available at hardware stores. It can be cut into short lengths to make rollers. Oil the roller lightly to prevent sticking.

MAT BOARD Strips of mat board are helpful for rolling out even sheets of clay. Place a strip of mat board on each side of the clay to be rolled, rolling the clay in between with the roller ends resting on the mat board (see "Rolling Sheets of Clay" on page 23). Mat board is a good thickness for many projects, making a nice heavy gauge for finished projects.

PLAYING CARDS Playing cards can be used in the same way as mat board to roll out sheets of clay, but you can adjust the thickness of the clay by varying the number of cards. Place an equal number of cards on each side of the clay to be rolled (see "Rolling Sheets of Clay" on page 23). Cards can also be used as tools to move clay and to cut clay edges.

CRAFT OR PARING KNIFE Use a knife to score the clay, cut strips of clay, or cut out clay shapes. The point of the knife is ideal for drilling or enlarging holes in dried clay.

TISSUE OR MAT CUTTING BLADE Sharp, long blades give you a straight cutting edge. Polymer clay suppliers sell different types of blades, including wavy-shaped blades. Mat cutting blades are available at art supply stores.

NEEDLE TOOL OR TOOTHPICK Needle tools, which are used by ceramic artists, are perfect for poking holes, attaching clay, and working in small areas. Round toothpicks serve the same purpose, but can be left in place and fired with the clay. This is helpful when making beads or delicate loops.

STRAWS Plastic drinking straws or small cocktail straws cut perfect holes in metal clay. Dip the straw in olive oil to prevent the clay from sticking to it. Straws also make good forms for tubular shapes.

SMALL PAINTBRUSHES Paintbrushes are useful for applying slip and water. Smooth delicate, hard-to-reach areas with a pointed brush, or large flat areas with a wide brush.

CLAY SHAPERS Rubber-tipped clay shapers can be used instead of a paintbrush. Clay will not collect on them as much as it does in the bristles of a paintbrush. Use them to texture clay and to apply slip. They are useful for repairs and for blending fresh clay into seams. Art supply stores and polymer clay suppliers sell different shapes and sizes of clay shapers.

PMC RULER A PMC ruler is marked to gauge clay shrinkage after firing. You can also use the edge of the PMC ruler or a standard ruler as a guide for cutting straight lines in the clay.

PLASTIC WRAP Wrap unused clay in plastic to help keep it fresh.

SMALL CONTAINERS Small bottles, film canisters, and pill bottles are handy for storing extra clay, for mixing and storing slip, and for collecting scraps of dry clay.

CLAY CUTTERS Clay pattern cutters are available at art supply and craft stores. Klay Kutters are small clay cutters manufactured by Kemper Tools. They are available in a variety of shapes and sizes and feature a plunger that pushes the clay out if it sticks in the cutter. You can also use small cookie cutters to cut clay shapes.

TEXTURING TOOLS You can find metal- and leather-stamping tools in jewelry and leather supply stores and catalogs. The pointed end of a knitting needle, kitchen utensils, pieces of hardware, fabric, lace, buttons, and other found objects create great textures on clay. Rubber stamps made for paper can also be used to add texture to clay.

BABY WIPES Keep these handy for wiping residue off your fingers. I find they work better than water because they keep your hands moist and prevent the clay from sticking to your hands. I sometimes place one over clay to keep it from drying out when I'm working and am too busy to wrap the clay.

SANDING AND BUFFING TOOLS Most of the tools traditionally used for silver and gold finish work are applicable to metal clay, such as tumblers, scratch brushes, needle tools, sandpapers and pads, buffing cloths, fingernail files, and pumice stones (see "Finishing Fired Metal Clay" on page 33). Sandpapers, buffing cloths, and files can also be used to refine dried metal clay pieces before they are fired (see "Finishing Unfired Metal Clay" on page 27).

Cork Clay

Cork clay is a product you can use to make bead cores or other hollow forms. You can roll this clay between your hands to make shapes and sculpt it as you would any other clay or papier-mâché product. Allow the forms to air dry for several days or speed the process by putting them in a dehydrator or on a coffee-mug/candle warmer. Metal clay can then be applied around the form and fired.

Use a kiln to fire any project formed around cork clay. An enclosed kiln will contain the flames and smoke that emit from cork clay as it burns. It helps to use a slow ramp speed (see page 28), as that will allow any remaining moisture in the cork clay to dissipate as it heats up. This will help prevent cracks or split seams in your metal clay pieces. The projects in this book that involve cork clay suggest a ramp speed of 1500°F/per hour, instead of full speed, on a programmable kiln.

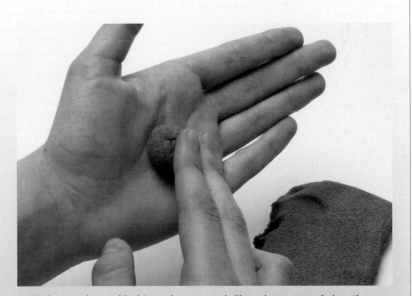

Cork clay can be molded into shapes much like other types of clay. If needed, use a little water to moisten the clay to keep it soft and pliable as you work.

Basic Techniques

ONCE YOU KNOW a few basic techniques, working with metal clay is fairly easy. Rolling clay into uniform sheets, shaping basic clay forms, and making attachments are fundamental skills used over and over again with metal clay. Knowing how to sand and refine dried clay prior to firing will result in beautifully finished jewelry pieces.

NOTRE DAME WINDOW NECKLACE #1 *by Shahasp Valentine*
Metal clay is a malleable, responsive material, making it easy to create even intricate textures such as on this pendant inspired by a cathedral window. (Photo by the artist.)

KEEPING CLAY HYDRATED

I've listed this as the first technique for a reason. I find that the biggest challenge faced by those who work with metal clay is controlling the moisture level in the clay. Keeping the clay soft and pliable (not too dry and not wet and sticky) requires paying attention to the clay as you work. Some people are nervous when they first open the clay and fear it will dry out too quickly as they are working on a project. You can relax if you attend to your clay, keeping it moist and becoming familiar with the different stages of workability as it relates to your climate. You will want to pace yourself and control the drying of the clay as you progress through a project. There are different stages of workability as the clay goes from fresh and moist to bone dry.

There are several ways to keep clay hydrated. You can periodically mist the clay with water using a spray bottle, or you can sprinkle water on the clay. Work with small pieces of clay and leave the rest inside a sealed container with a small damp sponge to keep it from drying out. I always dab a few drops of water on my unused clay and keep it wrapped in plastic wrap at my workspace. PMC Supply offers innovative containers called the Clay Vault™ and ClaySafe™ that are designed to be opened and used one-handed, allowing you to work uninterrupted without stopping to wrap the clay. Olive oil or Badger Balm also help to keep your hands and the clay from drying out while you work, adding another measure of control.

Even if your clay does dry out, it's not too late. Dried clay can be rehydrated, and scraps can be used to make slip; nothing is lost or wasted. If the clay becomes too dry, add drops of water to it and leave it wrapped for a few hours or overnight. Bone-dry clay may take longer (several days) to rehydrate, but it can still be reconditioned into soft clay.

WORKING WITH FRESH, WET CLAY

Fresh, moist clay right out of the package is easy to shape and manipulate. Make delicate components such as loops, braids, and fine details at this stage, while the clay is soft and flexible. Pieces of wet clay can be attached to each other by simply applying water. Slip can also be used sparingly to join pieces of wet clay, but be cautious: Cleaning up slip around joints is tricky on fresh clay, as the clay piece will easily become misshapen or lose texture if it is too wet. With a little practice, you can learn to judge when the clay is firm enough to use slip.

ROLLING SHEETS OF CLAY

Place a lump of metal clay on your work surface and use a roller to form the clay into a sheet. If the clay sticks, rub a small amount of olive oil or balm on the work surface and the roller. If the clay cracks and splits, it may be too dry. Mist the surface with water, wait a minute, and try rolling the clay again. If you see any air bubbles form as you roll out the clay, pierce them with a needle tool or toothpick and smooth the clay with your fingers or the roller. Many projects in this book were made with sheets of clay. To roll out an even thickness of clay, you can use either two strips of mat board or several playing cards as guides.

MAKING ROPES AND LOOPS

Use fresh clay to make ropes or "snakes" out of clay. Thicker ropes can be used to make sturdy loops for pendants; very fine ropes can be used as decorative elements on a piece. To make a snake of clay, pinch off a small amount of clay and roll the clay on your work surface using the fingertips of both hands. As you roll, move along the length of the snake, applying even pressure with your fingers for a uniform thickness. As you apply

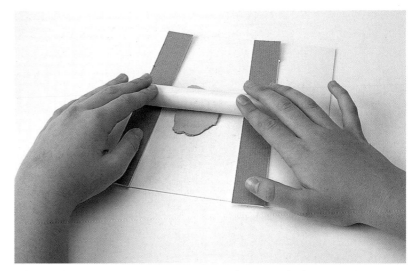

Roll the clay between two strips of mat board to get a thickness of about 1.5 mm. This thickness is sturdy enough for most metal clay projects such as pendants and rings. From there, you can use your eye to judge the thickness.

Tim McCreight developed this clever alternative method. Place the clay between two stacks of playing cards and roll it to the thickness of the cards: five to six cards on each side for thicker sheets, four cards for medium thickness, and two to three cards for thin sheets.

downward pressure, push or coax the clay away from the center outwards to lengthen it. If the rope gets too long to manage, cut it into shorter pieces and continue rolling until you have the thickness you need. Spray the clay rope with water as needed to keep it moist. If you leave a rope of clay while working on another element, keep it covered with a wet towel or plastic wrap.

Attaching clay ropes or rings to unfired clay pieces eliminates the need to solder. To make a loop or small ring of clay, form a small, thin rope of clay into a circle. Cut the ends cleanly to make a butt joint. Wet the ends with water and press together to seal. Let the loop dry a bit and attach to the unfired metal clay piece with thick slip. Applying more slip to the piece as it dries will ensure a secure bond.

CREATING TEXTURE   One of the nicest features of metal clay is that it will pick up details from textured objects. There is no end to what you can use to add texture to clay. Fabric, lace, rubber stamps, and metal- or leatherworking tools all create interesting textures. Objects found around the house or even in nature provide plenty of sources for great textures. You can also press the clay into a mold to create texture. Use a bit of olive oil to keep the tools or material from sticking to the clay.

MAKING CLAY ATTACHMENTS   When the clay is still fresh and wet you can make attachments by simply adding water and pressing the pieces together. As soon as clay is firm enough to handle, you can add attachments of fresh clay with slip, syringe clay, or water. The clay should be dry enough to keep its shape but still have enough moisture to make the attachments adhere easily.

NAVIGATIONAL AID #32
by Robert Dancik
The textures created in the metal clay portion of this pendant echo the design scratched into Faux Bone™, an innovative product Robert developed. (Photo by Douglas Foulke.)

Kitchen tools, cookie molds, rubber stamps, fabric, lace, found objects, and buttons are just a few possible objects and materials you can use to add texture to metal clay.

Slip, Paste & Syringe Clay

Slip is clay that has been watered down to the consistency of thick cream. It acts like a glue to attach either wet or dry clay elements to each other. To make your own slip, mix clay with distilled water and a few drops of vinegar in a small bottle or lidded container. The vinegar will keep mold from growing on the clay. Dry bits of clay or clay shavings can also be used to make slip. If you're in a hurry, you can mix slip right on your work surface with moist clay and water. Use a clay shaper to blend soft clay and water to make a smooth paste or slip. Mark your slip jars to remember which type of clay they contain. Always keep oil paste, which is a different product, separate from slip; do not mix the two.

Paste is basically premixed slip. It's a nice product to use because it has been formulated to be an ideal consistency, which is sometimes hard to achieve when you make your own. If you want to make an attachment such as joining a bail to a pendant, use paste in conjunction with syringe clay for a secure attachment.

I keep syringe-type clay at my workspace alongside my basic tools. The consistency is perfect for making attachments, filling gaps, or strengthening weak areas. Like clay, it has enough body to fill an area, yet it is soft enough to be smoothed into joints and cracks like a thick slip. I routinely add this to joints as a piece dries to make sure the joints are solid and secure. Store the open syringe clay in a cup of water or a floral tube to keep it hydrated. Return the syringe to the cup or tube of water immediately after use.

You can use syringe clay to make attachments, or, if the clay has enough moisture in it, just a little water or slip may be sufficient.

WORKING WITH DRY CLAY

You can tell that metal clay is dry by the way it looks and feels. Clay becomes lighter in color as moisture evaporates. Damp clay is cool to the touch. The type of clay used, the thickness of the clay, and the humidity of the climate all determine the length of time it takes metal clay to dry.

Small pieces of rolled paper, cardboard, or straws can be used to prop and support the clay as it dries. Three-dimensional forms, such as beads, can be propped up to dry with toothpicks or skewers stuck into a Styrofoam block or in a cup filled with sand.

LEATHER-HARD CLAY The stage between moist, flexible clay and bone-dry clay is called *leather hard*. The piece looks and feels dry and will retain its shape and form when handled, but it still has enough moisture to be joined to other pieces. You can "glue" two pieces of leather-hard clay together with slip or syringe clay. If you have enough surface area to scratch a few lines in the clay, score the pieces to help secure the attachment.

You can refine or make holes bigger in a leather-hard piece with a pin vise (a small tool that holds drill bits to manually drill holes) or the tip of a craft knife. I find the knife is less likely to tear or break the clay, because it "shaves" the clay without catching or dragging as it is twirled around. Be careful not to make the hole too close to the edge of the clay or the clay will split.

BONE-DRY CLAY Clay that is completely dry is called *bone dry*. Pieces can be easily handled at this stage and sanded to refine. Smooth the surface of a bone-dry piece with water to further refine it before firing. Clay elements (wet or dry) can still be added to bone-dry clay, but it may be necessary to apply several layers of slip or syringe clay to create a strong connection.

Finished pieces will dry quickly and evenly on a wire rack or on a sponge, which help air circulation. Small thin pieces will dry quickly (approximately 30 minutes). Larger pieces of clay can take a few hours or more to dry. If you want to make sure a thick piece of clay is bone dry, you can leave it overnight or speed the drying time with heat.

To speed drying, you can use a hair dryer, food dehydrator, or mug warmer, although quick-drying methods may warp the clay. If the clay warps, flip it over as it dries. (You can also bend or flatten the metal after firing. Don't bend bone-dry clay; it will crack).

Twist the point of a craft knife to "drill" a hole in leather-hard clay. The blade of the knife shaves the clay away as the hole is enlarged.

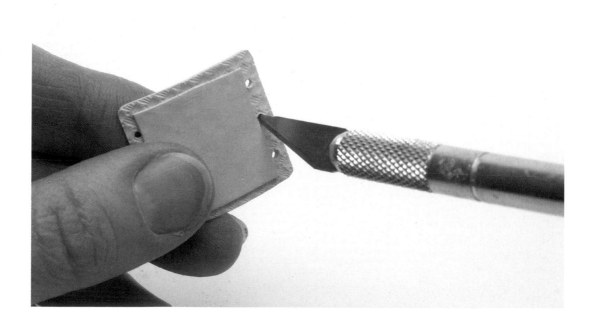

FINISHING UNFIRED METAL CLAY

Cleaning up and refining a piece before it is fired saves time and effort in the finishing process. Dry, unfired clay is fragile. Take care to hold and support the piece to avoiding causing stress that could break it.

Before beginning, determine how much refining needs to be done. Fine sandpapers are usually sufficient. Nail files are small and work very well to bevel or smooth edges. Use fine polishing papers or swabs for tight spots or to sand around small details.

After you have sanded a piece, you can smooth any hard-to-reach areas with a small paintbrush and water. Be careful not to remove textures with water; only a small amount is needed to soften edges. Damp cosmetic sponges work well to smooth the dried clay.

MAKING REPAIRS TO UNFIRED CLAY

Unfired clay can be repaired before firing. Brush water onto the broken pieces and then apply thin slip, paste, or syringe clay. Press the broken pieces together and let the repaired clay dry. Carefully add more slip, paste, or syringe clay to fill in any cracks that appear while the clay dries. As a final step, smooth the repaired joint with a brush dipped in water.

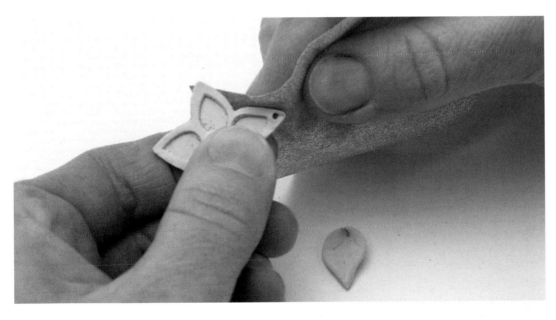

Flexible polishing papers allow you to sand around tight spots to create smooth edges.

FAR LEFT: To repair broken pieces of unfired clay, brush water and thin slip or paste on the broken pieces, then press them together to dry.

LEFT: As the repaired piece dries, add more slip or paste to fill in any cracks that appear.

METAL CLAY needs to be fired long enough at a hot enough temperature to fuse the metal particles properly. Under-fired pieces are brittle and will snap like chalk. Overheating will melt the metal; never fire metal clay above the melting temperatures of 1762°F for fine silver, 1945°F for 24-karat gold, and 1931°F for 22-karat gold. Each type of clay has different firing possibilities. Refer to the firing chart on page 32 to make sure you fire your metal clay pieces correctly.

It's best to let metal clay pieces dry thoroughly before firing. If any moisture remains in the clay during firing, steam will expand and escape, causing cracks in the clay. Hidden air bubbles trap steam, which could burst though the piece.

FIRING DEVICES

Just as metal clay products and accessories have been developed and improved since metal clay was first introduced, firing methods have also been evolving. There are new firing devices and products that make firing easier and less expensive than it had been in the past. The type of clay used, the materials you will be firing with the clay, and how many pieces you plan to fire will determine the firing device best suited for your needs. Here is an overview of each type of firing device and the advantages of each. (You can also fire certain metal clays with a butane torch; see page 30.)

SMALL ELECTRONIC KILNS Following the rise in popularity of metal clay, suppliers began offering small kilns specifically for the purpose of firing metal clay. In fact, a few of these kilns feature pre-programmed settings for metal clay. With the touch of a button, you can fire your clay without having to manually set the temperature and time. Most metal clay suppliers carry kilns and accessories, which makes the job of shopping for the right kiln much easier.

Even if the kiln isn't made especially for metal clay, a programmable kiln is easy to use. Use the chart on page 32 to manually set the temperature and time applicable for a certain type of clay or project. Set a ramp speed if needed (see "Ramp Speed," below). (This is the rate at which the kiln heats up as described below.)

Large kilns commonly used for ceramics, even if they have a controller, fluctuate quite a bit in temperature. The temperature and time need to be consistent for metal clay to

Ramp Speed

Ramp speed is the length of time it takes to reach a certain temperature. Controlling the ramp speed is particularly useful when combining metal clay with materials such as glass, ceramics, and cork clay. Slower ramping reduces the stresses on metal clay or other heat-sensitive materials, resulting in fewer cracks, splits, or ruined projects. The projects in the book give specific ramping instructions when necessary.

Using a kiln made for firing metal clay allows you to easily control the time and temperature needed for a successful project.

sinter (or fuse) properly. A better solution would be to use a small enameling kiln outfitted with a pyrometer to kiln fire the clay. Many metal clay artists successfully fire metal clay with this type of kiln.

ULTRA-LITE BEEHIVE KILN© This small electric kiln is an inexpensive alternative to a full-sized electronic kiln. It can be used to fire metal clay and enamels, to fuse glass, or for the technique of Keum-boo (see page 135). Accessories for firing and a temperature-control unit are available for use with this unit, making it a versatile firing device.

SPEEDFIRE™ CONE The SpeedFire Cone is an economical firing unit that is fueled with a commonly available propane fuel tank. This firing device fires all types of metal clay, and features a pyrometer for accurate temperature readings. It can be used to fire enamels and glass beads with metal clay as well. This unit allows you to fire larger pieces than would be possible with a small butane torch (see page 30). The SpeedFire Cone is manufactured by PMC Supply and is available through several metal clay suppliers.

USING A KILN

Prepare the metal clay pieces for firing. Make sure that everything that is being fired together is compatible temperature-wise. Use the lowest temperature for a longer length of time if you are combining different types of clay or using materials that require lower firing temperatures.

Set the clay pieces on a hard Solderite™ pad (available from metal clay suppliers) or a kiln shelf. Arrange the pieces so that they are close together but not touching.

Load the kiln with the shelves on which the metal clay pieces have been arranged. You can use small kiln bricks to stack multiple shelves

LEFT: The Ultra-Lite Beehive Kiln heats quickly and evenly, providing the ideal temperature for firing metal clay.

The SpeedFire Cone is a portable, temperature-controlled device that can fire up to 100 grams of clay at a time.

Kiln Safety

Be sure to follow these safety tips when using any type of kiln or firing device:
- Read the kiln manufacturer's instructions carefully before using your kiln.
- Do not fire the kiln hotter than is recommended for the metal clay.
- Do not leave the kiln unattended while firing.
- Do not touch the sides of the kiln while it is heated.
- Fire in a well-ventilated area.
- Do not bring anything into contact with the heating elements and unplug the kiln after firing.
- Wear safety glasses when opening the door of the hot kiln.
- Always fire your metal clay items on a kiln shelf, not the floor of the kiln.

You can place items directly on a kiln shelf or rest rounded pieces on a fiber blanket (top) or bed of vermiculite (bottom right).

in the kiln. Place same-sized blocks in each corner for stability as you stack the shelves. Make sure that nothing is touching the thermocouple (a small probe sticking out of the back wall of the kiln that controls the temperature).

Round or shaped pieces need to be cradled in a fireproof material as they are fired. I prefer to use refractory ceramic fiber. Also known as a "ceramic fiber blanket" or "doll prop," it is used for making porcelain dolls and is available in ceramic stores.

Some artists use other materials for supporting metal clay during firing. Small terracotta pots filled with vermiculite or alumina hydrate can be used to support round or dimensional objects. Vermiculite is commonly found in gardening supply stores, and is economical to use. Alumina hydrate works well to support pieces as it is very fine and heavy; however, use caution with the loose powder. Because the powder is very fine and can damage your lungs if you breathe it in, you must wear a dust mask or respirator while using it.

Load the kiln and set the controls for the proper time and temperature needed to fire

the metal clay. Refer to the manufacturer of the kiln for operating instructions. After the firing is complete, unplug the kiln and let it cool down. You can let the kiln cool slowly or open the door to cool it down quickly. Leave the door shut if the project specifies a slow cooling time.

Remove the shelves with heat-proof pads or tongs. Pieces without stones or inclusions can be quenched in water to cool. Stones, glass, or ceramics may shatter if cooled too quickly, so let these materials cool slowly at room temperature.

BUTANE TORCH FIRING

Low-fire types of metal clay can be fired with a small handheld torch instead of a kiln. These are the same kind of torches used to caramelize sugar for crème brûlée. Butane fuel for the torch—the same that's used to fill cigarette lighters—is available at grocery or variety stores. Torch firing works for small pieces (smaller than a silver dollar and/or projects made with less than 25 grams of metal clay). You can fire PMC3, Art Clay Silver Standard, and Art Clay Silver 650/1200 with a butane torch. To fire metal clay with a torch, follow the steps on the following page.

Repairing Fired Metal Clay

Fired metal objects sometimes break due to a weak joint, or crack during firing. Fired metal clay can be repaired using fresh clay and thick slip or paste and then refired. Sometimes it's tricky to get slip or paste to stick to the metal. You can apply a thick layer to hold the pieces together and then refine the piece after firing, with a metal file. Art Clay Silver Oil Paste works very well to join fired pieces. Oil Paste can also be used if you decide to add elements to fired metal clay objects.

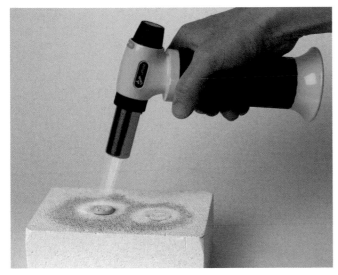

1 Place the completely dry metal clay piece on a firebrick or soldering block. Make sure you're working on a heat-proof table and away from anything combustible. If a piece contains a stone, place the stone face down on the surface. Use only stones that are strong enough to withstand high temperatures.

Fill the torch with butane. Ignite the torch and hold it over the piece at a very close range—about 1.5 inches away.

2 Keep the torch moving slowly over the piece. A small flame and smoke will briefly appear as the binder burns out.

3 Keep the torch moving and watch as the piece glows red-orange. It's easier to see the orange color in a darker room, away from bright light or sunlight. Keep the metal glowing with even heat for proper fusing, and at the same time avoid melting the piece, which can happen quickly if you are not paying attention.

4 As soon as the piece begins glowing red-orange, start timing. Fire for at least an additional 1.5 to 2 minutes for a small piece. Large pieces can take a few minutes longer, up to 5 minutes. These are minimum times; it doesn't hurt to fire any piece longer. Keep the piece glowing orange the whole time, all the while moving the torch evenly over it. If the piece starts to shimmer or looks shiny, the silver is beginning to melt. Quickly pull the torch back. Continue firing, adjusting the torch distance as needed. After firing, turn off the torch and let the piece air cool.

Firing Charts

THE TIMES LISTED below are minimums. It will not harm the metal to fire it longer. Doing so allows you to fire different types of clays together. However, if one piece requires a lower temperature because it contains stones, ceramics, or cork clay, for example, fire all pieces at the lower temperature. Refer to the instructions on page 30 for torch firing.

PRECIOUS METAL CLAY FIRING CHART

Clay type/Properties	Recommended firing method	Kiln firing temperature and minimum time	Shrinkage
PMC STANDARD Very smooth clay. Good for small projects when shrinkage is desired, such as charms, pendants, small sculptures.	Kiln	1650°F for 2 hours	25–30%
PMC+ Strong clay. Good all-purpose clay for bracelets, earrings, pins, beads, enameling.	Kiln	1650°F for 10 min. 1560°F for 20 min. 1470°F for 30 min.	10–15%
PMC3 Very strong clay. Can be fired with stones, such as garnets, moonstones, and hematite; glass; ceramics; and sterling silver findings. Good for rings and pieces requiring strength.	Kiln or torch	1650°F for 5 min. 1290°F for 10 min. 1200°F for 20 min. 1110°F for 30 min.	10–12%
PMC GOLD Good for making pendants, charms, earrings, rings. Can be layered or fired with silver metal clay.	Kiln or torch	1650°F for 10 min. 1560°F for 30 min. 1380°F for 60 min. 1290°F for 90 min.	14–19%

ART CLAY SILVER FIRING CHART

Clay type/Properties	Recommended firing method	Kiln firing temperature and minimum time	Shrinkage
ART CLAY SILVER STANDARD Strong all-purpose clay. Good for pins, pendants, sculpted forms, beads.	Kiln or torch	1600°F for 10 min. 1560°F for 20 min. 1472°F for 30 min.	8–12%
ART CLAY SILVER SLOW DRY Good for rings and detailed pieces. Allows longer working time (helpful in dry climates).	Kiln or torch	1600°F for 10 min. 1560°F for 20 min. 1472°F for 30 min.	8–12%
ART CLAY SILVER 650/1200 Low-firing clay. Fires with sterling silver findings, glass, ceramics, and stones such as moonstone, garnet, and hematite.	Kiln or torch	1472°F for 5 min. 1200°F for 30 min.	8–9%
ART CLAY GOLD 22-karat-gold clay.	Kiln	1813°F for 60 min.	15%

AFTER FIRING, silver metal clay has a powdery white surface. Gold metal clay is a matte light yellow color. The white or light yellow appearance is caused by light reflecting at different angles on tiny silver particles that stick up like the bristles of a brush. As the particles are flattened, or burnished, the surface begins to reflect the bright silver. The more the surface is refined, the brighter and shinier the silver will become. With a few modifications, the traditional tools and techniques used for silver and gold finishing work are applicable to metal clay.

BURNISHING

Provided you don't have to file or sand away imperfections in your fired piece, the first step in finishing a piece of fired metal clay is burnishing, which compresses the surface particles and brings out the luster in the silver. There are a variety of tools you can use, including brass or stainless steel brushes and other tools made specifically for burnishing metal.

BRASS BRUSHING Brass brushing, which is also known as "scratch brushing," is my favorite method for burnishing metal clay pieces. It is the first, and sometimes last, step I follow in finishing a piece.

Brass brushes work very well for achieving a matte metal finish and for finishing pieces with deeply textured surfaces. Jewelry suppliers and metal clay suppliers sell brushes for this purpose. I prefer to brush the piece with a dry brush until the metal starts to shine. Some choose instead to use gentle soap and running water to lubricate the brush, or to brush the metal with a bit of baking soda and water to clean the piece. The soap or baking soda will help if you are going to use a patina solution (see page 35) to reduce the amount of patina retained in the porous surface of the silver metal. It also keeps the brass brush from depositing particles, which sometimes imparts

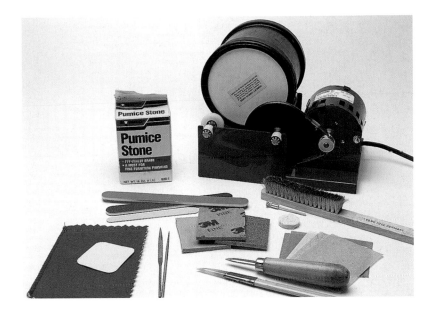

ABOVE: Finishing tools, including a tumbler, burnishing tools, sandpapers, and polishing cloths.

LEFT: Burnishing a piece with a brass brush flattens the silver particles and brings out a satin finish.

a golden cast to the silver. Small scratch brushes available for Dremel® or flexible-shaft tools are useful for small areas. Many of the projects in this book were finished with a brass brush alone. If you prefer a mirror shine, you will want to follow with fine sandpapers and burnishing tools. Some artists prefer burnishing with stainless steel brushes, which produce a slightly different finish than brass. Other choices include flexible-shaft tools or bench lathes fitted with a rotary brush or polishing disk attachment.

USING BURNISHING TOOLS Stainless steel burnishing tools are available at jewelry or metal clay suppliers. Using a stainless steel burnishing tool is usually the final step in finishing a piece. It's mentioned here because high spots can be burnished with a burnishing tool immediately following scratch brushing to complete a highly textured piece. Flat pieces can be polished with progressively finer papers first, before using a burnishing tool as the final step. You can use other household items such as metal knitting needles, stainless steel kitchen spoons, or paper clips to burnish the metal, especially in tight spots.

To burnish an item, hold it firmly and apply pressure while rubbing the surface with the tool. The tool will compress and flatten the metal particles for a high shine.

TUMBLING Another method for burnishing metal clay is to use a jewelry or rock tumbler. Tumbling also hardens the metal for a stronger finished product. Jewelry supply catalogs and metal clay suppliers offer small tumblers for use with metal clay. Mini rotary tumblers are inexpensive and save time if you will be finishing a large number of pieces. Use a professional-grade tumbler, not a toy model. Fill the tumbler with stainless steel mixed shot and burnishing compound liquid. The mixed shot contains a variety of shapes to burnish all of the nooks and crannies of the metal surface. Hollow pieces such as beads can be strung on a wire prior to tumbling to prevent shot from being trapped in the bead.

Follow the manufacturer's instructions for filling and operating the tumbler. Prepare your fired metal pieces first by brass brushing and tumble the pieces for about an hour. Check the pieces periodically and remove them when they reach the desired shine and finish.

Vibratory tumblers and magnetic tumblers are two other types of tumblers that work very well for burnishing metal clay.

FILING AND SANDING

Although you may be satisfied to finish a piece with a brass brush alone, the added steps of filing and sanding allow you to refine the surface, soften edges, and remove scratches.

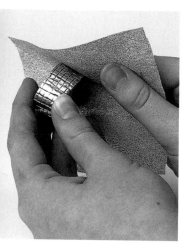

For a mirror-like finish, sand the piece with fine sandpapers, then buff with a jewelry-polishing cloth for more shine.

Brushing simply burnishes the surface, whereas filing and sanding actually remove metal as well as burnish. This can be done at any step along the way. As a rule of thumb, files and rougher sandpaper grits are used early in the finishing process to remove high spots or to round off areas of unwanted metal. Using progressively finer sandpapers at the end of the finishing process will give the metal a mirror-like finish. You will find that it is a back-and-forth process until you achieve the finish you are pleased with.

METAL FILES Small, pointed jewelry files are used to finish rough or hard-to-reach areas. They are available in sets from jewelrymaking or modelmaking suppliers. File the metal in one direction, then follow with sandpapers (see below) to remove scratches. If you smooth and finish a metal clay piece well before firing, this step may be unnecessary.

NAIL FILES Filing and buffing files made for fingernails are available in different shapes and grits at variety stores or beauty supply stores. These can be used in the same manner on fired metal as they are used on unfired clay. Sand the edges of the metal with a file, followed by progressively finer sandpapers.

SANDING PADS AND PAPERS Flexible sponge sanding pads graded from medium to micro-fine can be used to finish both unfired and fired metal clay. Rough grits will scratch the fired metal; this grit should be used if you are trying to remove metal or smooth a very rough area. Move progressively from the coarse pads to the finer grits to remove scratches and give the metal a smooth finish. Follow with polishing papers if desired. Wet/dry sandpapers and polishing supplies are available from hardware or automotive stores.

Polishing papers are thin, flexible sheets that are used for extra-fine polishing. You can cut the papers into small pieces to sand tight or curved areas. Create a mirror finish on metal clay by starting with the most abrasive paper and moving progressively to the finest paper. These papers are sold by jewelry suppliers and auto supply shops.

Polishing swabs are yet another tool for sanding and burnishing recessed or hard-to-reach areas. They are available in a variety of grits and sizes.

BUFFING

After you have sanded a piece with fine papers, you can buff it with buffing pads or jewelry-polishing cloths for more shine. Pieces can also be polished using a rotary machine or flexible-shaft tool fitted with a muslin buffing wheel and jeweler's rouge.

ADDING A PATINA TO METAL CLAY

The same surface treatments that are traditionally used on sterling or fine silver can be applied to finished metal clay. Patina solutions, which are available through jewelry suppliers, add color or darken the metal through the process of oxidation. Experiment with different solutions and make sample chips of fired metal to keep a record of different patinas. Because fired metal clay is porous, it's best to tumble or burnish before soaking in a patina solution.

Liver of sulfur is a common solution used to oxidize a piece. Be sure to follow safety precautions, work in a well-ventilated area, and wear gloves to protect your skin. Liver of sulfur should be kept away from eating areas and disposed of after use. Check with local authorities about proper disposal methods in your area.

To begin the patina process, dissolve a few chips of dry liver of sulfur in hot water. Heat the silver pieces by running them under hot water first. Use a wire to dip the pieces into the solution and watch as the color moves from golden yellow to blue and finally to blue-black. Remove the pieces from the solution when you like the color. Rinse the silver under cold water and polish with fine sandpapers or buffing pads to remove the patina from the raised areas.

ABOVE: THE SQUIRE'S SHIELD *by Kelly Russell* Kelly used liver of sulfur to apply a golden patina to the metal clay centerpiece of this striking necklace. (Photo by Robert Diamante.)

LEFT: Dipping the silver piece into the patina solution with a wire allows you to check the piece frequently until the desired color of patina is achieved.

BOTTOM LEFT: Buffing the patina off of the surface of the metal leaves the recessed areas dark; this adds contrast and emphasizes textures.

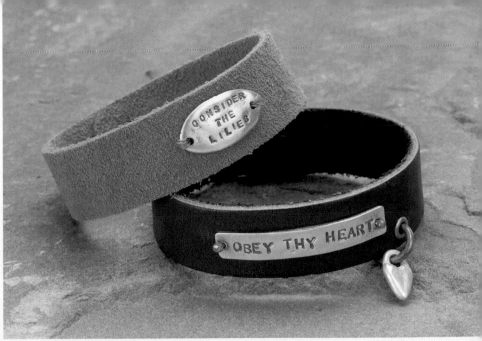

Creative
Connections

Mixed media jewelry incorporates a variety of nontraditional materials and merges them in unexpected ways. Fabric, leather, stones, plastic, and found objects can be combined with fired metal clay using rivets or wire-wrapping. Sewing and crocheting are other creative ways to combine metal clay with unusual materials. Working with such materials allows you to be creative with metal clay and encourages you to think beyond traditional techniques.

Embellishing Leather & Suede

ALPHABET STAMPS allow you to personalize silver with a message or name—a favorite technique with metal clay. Here, the traditional skill of riveting leather is used to attach a personalized silver plaque to a leather wristband. A premade wristband makes this a quick-and-easy project. If you have leatherworking skills, you can make your own customized cuff, setting snaps and rivets to make a closure.

TO MAKE ONE LEATHER WRISTBAND, YOU WILL NEED:

- PMC+
- Basic metal clay supplies
- Small letter stamps
- Tissue blade
- Narrow leather wristband (Silver Creek Leather Co.)
- Leather shears (Tandy Leather Factory)
- Eyelet and setter
- Leather hole punch (Tandy Leather Factory)
- Rawhide or plastic mallet (Tandy Leather Factory)
- Punch board (Tandy Leather Factory)
- Two 20-gauge copper rivets
- Awl or needle tool
- Wire cutters (hardware-store type)
- Ball-peen or rounded hammer
- Bench block (Volcano Arts)
- Jump ring to attach dangle

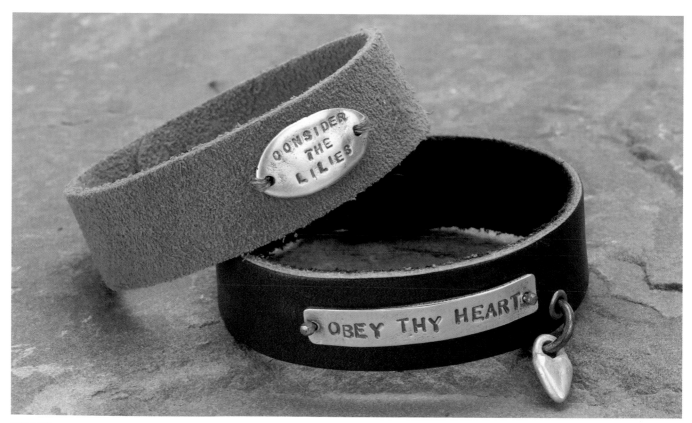

LEATHER AND SUEDE WRISTBANDS *by Sherri Haab*

1 Before working with the clay, arrange your letter stamps in order to spell a word or phrase. (This will help you stamp the letters quickly before the clay dries.) Pinch off a piece of clay and roll in into a smooth sheet, four or five cards thick. Stamp the letters into the clay.

2 Correct small flaws or marks left from the edges of the stamp using a clay shaper or a small paintbrush dampened with water.

3 Cut out the plaque with a blade, leaving room on each side of the letters for the rivets. Use a needle tool to make a small hole on each side of the shape. Let the piece dry, then softly sand the edges. Fire the piece at any of the temperatures recommended for PMC+.

You can also make a small charm dangle out of metal clay to attach to the wristband with an eyelet. For this project I made a heart shape with a hole in the top for hanging.

After firing, brass brush and polish the pieces with progressively finer sandpapers. Add a patina then buff the surface, leaving the letters darkened for contrast.

4 If you are adding a charm dangle, mark a spot on the wristband for placement and punch a hole that corresponds with the size of the eyelet using a hammer and punch. Hammer the punch into the leather on a punch board designed for leatherworking. Push the eyelet through and set with an eyelet setter and plastic or rawhide mallet. (This photo shows the type of hole punch used, the eyelets, and the eyelet setter.)

5 To attach the plaque to the leather wrist-band, place it in position and mark one of the holes onto the leather with a needle tool (you will add one rivet at a time). Punch a small hole in the leather with an awl or needle tool. Check to make sure the rivet fits through the hole.

6 Push the rivet all the way through the metal and the leather.

7 Making sure you have the proper length to rivet, use cutters to remove the excess wire and file the end flat. The cut length (or part you can see sticking out beyond the leather) should be half the diameter of the wire gauge. Use a wooden block (the bottom of the metal/wood block in this case) to support the piece as you file.

8 Place the wristband with the rivet onto a metal block. Use a ball-peen or rounded hammer to tap the rivet in a circular fashion around the filed end of the rivet, flip the piece over, and rivet the top of the rivet in the same fashion. Repeat the process to attach the other side of the plaque to the wristband with the remaining rivet. A good rivet will look like a rounded dome on top. This will hold the plaque in place on the leather.

9 Use a jump ring to attach the charm through the eyelet.

SUEDE VARIATION

Because suede is softer than leather, you can sew the plaque onto a suede wristband using a glover's needle and thread to match the suede. Hide the knots behind the plaque. (This plaque was made with clay flattened into an oval shape, about the size of a small coin. I formed the shape without using a template or cutters to give it a handmade look.)

Combining Silver & Acrylic

PLASTICS AND ACRYLIC create a contemporary look when combined with metal. In the past, acrylic was available only commercially in large sheets and in large quantities. Now, scrapbooking suppliers and variety stores carry small die-cut pieces of acrylic in a variety of colors and shapes. When creating a piece of jewelry that incorporates acrylic, you may want to base your design on an existing shape you find. Some other ideas you could try are to rivet a small metal clay charm to the center of a piece of acrylic, or to rivet smaller pieces of acrylic to a larger piece of metal clay.

TO MAKE ONE PENDANT, YOU WILL NEED:

- PMC+
- Syringe clay or thick slip
- Basic metal clay supplies
- Acrylic shape (Glass Effects: Mosaics by Heidi Grace Designs™)
- Small piece of Teflon paper
- Wet/dry sandpapers—320, 400, 600, 800, and 1000 grit (available from automotive supply shops)
- Nail file
- Brass texture sheet (or rubber stamp)
- Scissors
- Four finishing nails
- Center punch or needle tool
- Flexible-shaft tool or drill press
- Drill bit (same gauge as finishing nails)
- Tape
- Wire cutters (from hardware store, not for fine jewelry)
- Rubber block
- Small metal file
- Ball-peen hammer
- Bench block (Volcano Arts)
- Dust mask

ACRYLIC HEART PENDANT *by Sherri Haab*

1 To create metal clay sheets that will match the size of the acrylic shape after being fired (and shrinking), place the acrylic piece on a scanner or copier and increase the scale to 115 percent. Print the paper pattern and draw a simple shape (in this case a heart) in the center, which will be the window for the acrylic to shine through. Trace and cut the shape out of Teflon paper.

Roll out a sheet of metal clay that is three cards thick. Place the clay sheet over a texture sheet and roll once again to texture the clay. (If you use a rubber stamp, remember to oil the stamp.)

2 Lightly place the Teflon sheet pattern over the clay, being careful not to disturb the texture. Cut out the shape using the pattern as a guide. Use the point of a knife to cut the shape from the center.

3 Roll out another sheet of clay three cards thick for the back piece. This piece does not need a texture. Flip the Teflon pattern over so that the cutout is reversed or is the "mirror image" of the textured front piece. Cut out the shape as you did in step 2.

Let the front and back pieces dry. Refine the edges with sandpapers and a nail file, followed by a paintbrush and water to smooth.

4 Roll out a sheet of clay three cards thick to make a bail for hanging the pendant, then roll the clay over the texture sheet. Cut a narrow strip for the bail and wrap it loosely around a drinking straw. Cut the ends to form a butt joint and seal the joint with water. Let the bail dry on the straw. Slide the bail off the straw when dry and sand the edges.

5 Attach the bail to the top center of the textured front piece using thick slip or syringe clay. Let the piece dry on a raised surface (such as a wooden craft stick) with the bail hanging over the edge touching the table. After the piece dries, add more slip to the joint seam on the back of the bail. Smooth the seam with a clay shaper tool or a paintbrush. Let the seam dry.

Fire the pieces at any of the temperatures recommended for PMC+. Place the piece so that the bail hangs over the edge of the kiln shelf with the rest sitting flat on the shelf.

After firing, finish the pieces with a brass brush and polishing papers. Add a patina if desired. Buff and burnish the high surfaces with a buffing cloth and then burnishing tools.

6 Prepare the front piece for the riveting holes: Mark the placement of the holes by making a small indentation in each with a center punch (if you have one) or needle tool. This will serve as a guide for drilling. Using a flexible-shaft tool or drill press, drill through all four corners. The size of the hole should correspond to the gauge of the finishing nail so that the nail fits snugly in the hole.

7 Stack the front piece, the acrylic, and the back piece and tape the three pieces together. Don't worry about uneven edges; you can refine them later.

You're now ready to rivet the holes. This step through step 9 show one of the rivets being placed. Rivet one hole at a time, finishing each before starting the next.

Drill through the first hole and down through the acrylic and back piece. Push a finishing nail through the drilled layers.

8 Clip off the end of the nail, leaving just enough to form a rivet. The length of the part sticking out should be half the diameter of the nail. For nails this small, you will need only about 1 mm sticking out above the surface. (If you cut the end a bit long, you can file it down.) File the cut nail flat.

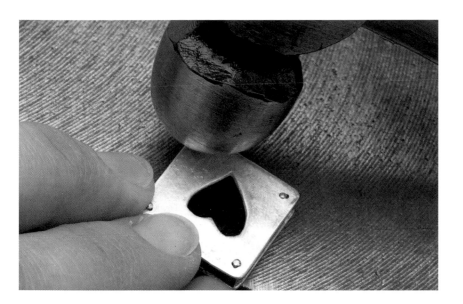

9 Place the piece on an anvil or metal block and gently tap around the end of the nail in a circular fashion. This will dome the rivet instead of smashing it flat. Don't pound so hard that you mar the silver or break the acrylic. Rivet each of the other nails.

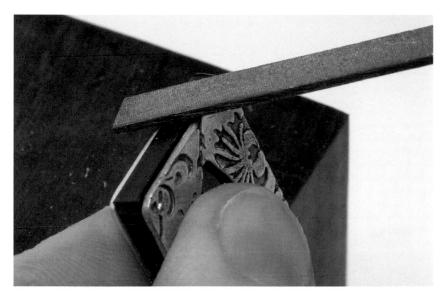

10 Finish the piece by filing and sanding all of the edges of the acrylic. (Be sure to wear a dust mask when sanding acrylic.) Start with a file for uneven areas, followed by 320-grit wet/dry sandpaper.

11 For a quick way to sand straight edges, lay a piece of sandpaper on a table, and sand, holding the pendant perpendicular to the table. Round the corners using the sandpaper or with a nail file. Sand with progressively finer sandpapers; this time in a shallow tray of water, which will prevent the acrylic dust from re-depositing on the edges and leaving a white buildup. Work with 400-, 600-, 800-, then 1000-grit sandpapers. After sanding, give the entire piece a final polish, buffing to a desired finish.

Complete the necklace by hanging the silver and acrylic pendant on a chain.

Polymer Clay

POLYMER CLAY is an oven-curing clay that is available in craft and hobby stores. It is made of particles of polyvinyl chloride (PVC) with a plasticizer added to make the material flexible and pliable. Polymer clay comes in many colors including metallic gold, silver, bronze, and pearl shades.

Polymer clay is an exciting material to use with metal clay, and there are several reasons why polymer clay and metal clay are compatible. Both materials are sculpted, textured, and molded with similar techniques and tools, and most polymer clay artists already own many of the tools that are used for working with metal clay. Polymer clay can be baked with prefired metal clay to decorate the metal. The ability to use polymer clay to add color to metal clay makes this art medium an attractive choice for artists who love working with metal clay.

There are a few things you should know before working with polymer clay. Polymer clay must be conditioned after opening the package. To condition the clay, knead it with your hands until it is soft and pliable. After conditioning the clay you can sculpt, roll, or shape the clay any way you would like. A favorite tool of polymer clay artists is a pasta roller. Pasta rollers make nice even sheets of

ABOVE: EXPERIMENTS
by Wendy Wallin Malinow
PMC, polymer clay, and pearls come together in a variety of unusual configurations. (Photo by Courtney Frisse.)

RIGHT: PODLING
by Kelly Russell
A PMC+ bezel provides the perfect setting for colorful polymer clay. The collar is made from labradorite beads crocheted around sterling silver. (Photo by Robert Diamante.)

clay in varying thicknesses. (This tool should be dedicated for use with polymer clay, as should all tools used with the clay. Polymer clay should not come into contact with any food-handling items.)

Baking polymer clay causes the particles to fuse into a hardened piece. When properly fused, the clay remains strong and flexible after baking. Bake polymer clay on a glass baking dish, ceramic tile, or clean piece of paper in an oven. For those who work with polymer clay frequently, it's best to use a toaster oven dedicated to polymer clay (or shrink plastic, not for food). Most polymer clay brands can be baked at 275°F for 30 minutes. Polymer clay emits toxic fumes if fired above the temperature given by the manufacturer, so read the manufacturer's instructions carefully. Let the clay cool in the oven for a stronger finished product.

Finish polymer clay similarly to metal clay, using progressively finer wet/dry sand-papers for a smooth finish, if desired. Polymer clay should always be added as the last element in a metal clay piece, and patinas should always be applied to metal before adding the polymer clay.

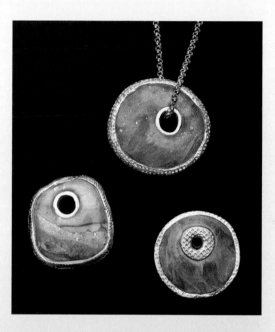

MOKUMÉ GANÉ DONUT BEADS *by Sherri Haab* Mokumé gané is a Japanese metal-working process, in which different kinds of metal are combined to simulate the look of wood grain. This effect can be imitated using layers of polymer clay, paint, and metal leaf.

SALTWATER CUFF *by Wendy Wallin Malinow* This vibrant cuff bracelet merges PMC3 with polymer clay to create a painterly effect. Beads are dangled from the piece as accents. (Photo by Courtney Frisse.)

Wire-Wrapping Beads & Rocks

RIVER ROCKS have a rough texture that contrasts nicely with shiny silver. If you have the right drill bit and a little patience, it's not hard to drill through river rocks to incorporate them into a jewelry design. Some rocks are harder to drill than others and may take more time to drill through. A diamond drill bit, which can also be used to drill through glass, works well when used in water to drill through the stones. In this project I made silver beads and charms and connected them to the rocks with silver wire.

TO MAKE ONE BRACELET, YOU WILL NEED:

- Art Clay Silver Standard or 650/1200 series
- Metal clay supplies
- Cork clay
- Small flat rocks
- Drill press or Dremel drill
- 1.5mm diamond twist drill bit (Rio Grande)

- Polymer clay
- Pinecones, twigs, or other textured items from nature
- 20-gauge half-hard round sterling silver wire
- Head pin
- Round-nose pliers
- Wire cutters

ROCK AND SILVER BRACELET *by Sherri Haab*

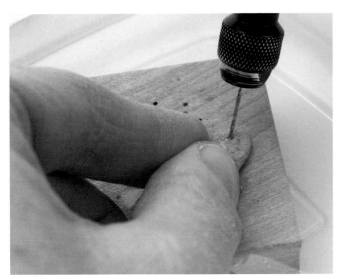

1 To drill a stone, use a diamond drill bit and drill the stone surrounded in water. This will help keep the heat from building up and the friction down (as the water lubricates and cleans debris) as you drill into the stone. Place the stone on a block of wood in a shallow container of water. Fill the container so that the surface of the rock is just below the level of the water. As you drill, only the drill bit will be in the water, not any part of the drill itself. To drill, start by holding the drill at an angle. Hold the rock firmly on the wood block with your other hand. With the drill on a high speed, touch the rock with the drill at a slight angle to "nick" a spot for the drill to follow with a hole.

2 Slowly come up with the drill while it is still drilling and in contact with the rock until the bit is perpendicular to the rock. Hold the drill steady as you drill straight down into the rock. As you are drilling a rock, remember to let the drill do the work, do not put pressure or force the bit or it will break. As the drill starts to go into the rock, pull back occasionally. This will allow the dust from the rock to clear out and let the water in to lubricate as the drill makes its way through the rock. Pull back just enough to let some water in, but not all the way out where you will lose your place. Some rocks take 20 minutes or more, so be patient. When you least expect it, the drill bit will suddenly hit the wood and you should be ready to pull back out with the drill (you don't want to drill all the way through the container by accident).

Drill two holes in each rock, one on each side. Set these aside as you make the rest of the elements for your bracelet.

3 Make a polymer clay texture mold to make silver charms: Roll out a pad of polymer clay. Press a textured pinecone or other item from nature into the clay to make a texture. Use a needle tool to make lines, in this case a stem for a flower shape. Bake the polymer clay piece in an oven at 275°F for 30 minutes.

4 After baking and cooling, the polymer clay mold can be used to make metal clay charms. Lightly oil the texture on the polymer and roll a pad of metal clay over the texture. Lift the metal clay off to reveal the textured image. Leave the edges rough for a natural look, or refine later. Pierce a hole on each side of the charm and let the piece dry.

5 Making beads: Make cork clay shapes to form the beads around. Let the shapes dry thoroughly. Roll out a pad of metal clay big enough to wrap around the cork form as shown.

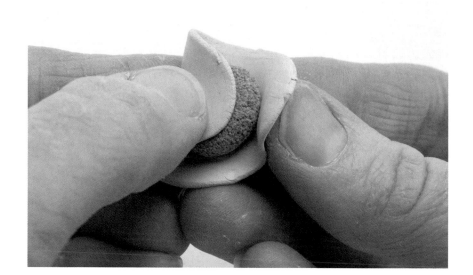

6 Seal the seams to fit the clay around the cork. Use a knife to cut off the excess clay. Don't stretch the clay too thin on the form or it will crack as it shrinks during firing.

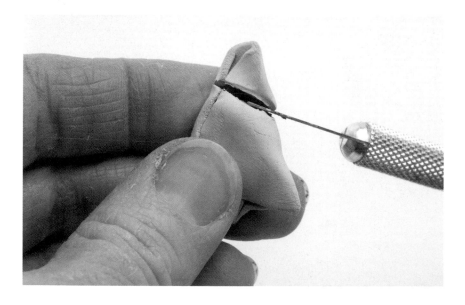

7 Use a needle tool to piece a hole on each end of the bead (pierce only through the clay layer; the cork will burn away during firing). Add details or textures to the bead if desired. Smooth all of the seams and repair any cracks that form as the bead dries.

Make small beads without cores to accent the design. Pierce a hole in the center of each. Make a loop and bar toggle out of metal clay (see "Embedding Collage Elements in Resin" on page 78 for directions) or purchase a clasp for the bracelet.

Fire the flat charms and beads in a kiln at 1472°F for 30 minutes at a ramp speed of 1500°F per hour. (Cradle the beads in vermiculite or a ceramic fiber blanket to support them during firing.) After firing, burnish and polish the silver to a desired finish.

8 To assemble the bracelet, use round-nose pliers to connect the rocks and silver pieces with wrapped wire loops. Include additional links of wrapped loops between the pieces to allow the pieces to swivel if needed. Thread a head pin through the toggle bar to add it to the bracelet. Add enough links to allow the bar to pass through the loop for the clasp.

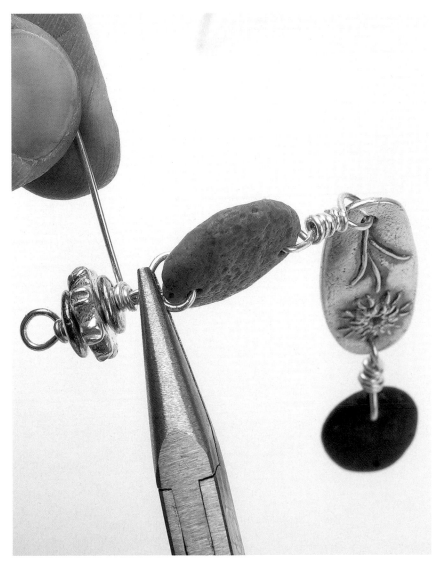

Designing a Figure with Silver & Beads

THIS PROJECT by Michelle Ross combines polymer clay with metal clay to create a whimsical figure. For a variation, you might want to make an animal or symbolic figure with found beads and findings to create a one-of-a-kind work of wearable art.

TO MAKE ONE PIN, YOU WILL NEED:

- PMC+
- Basic metal clay supplies
- Flexible Push Molds (#APM 24 "Miniature Dolls" for the hand and #APM 34 Art Doll Faces for the face; Sculpey/Polyform Products)
- 1/16-inch-wide steel knitting needle
- Hollow stir stick with a 1/8-inch hole
- One-inch marble (called a "shooter")
- ColorBox® Molding Mat ("Abstract Grids"; PMC Supply)
- Black polymer clay (Premo/Polyform Products)
- Water spray bottle

- Clay Texture Sheet ("Party Favors"; Sculpey/Polyform Products)
- Pearl Ex pigment powders (Jacquard Products)
- Syringe clay
- 20-gauge sterling silver wire (3 feet)
- Flat- or chain-nose pliers
- Assorted glass beads
- Round-nose pliers
- One jump ring (optional)
- Wire cutters
- Pin back
- Superglue (Zap-A-Gap®; optional)

WACKY WOMAN PINS
by Michelle Ross
Michelle is a well-known designer and TV craft demonstrator. She uses polymer clay in innovative ways and combines it with many types of media.

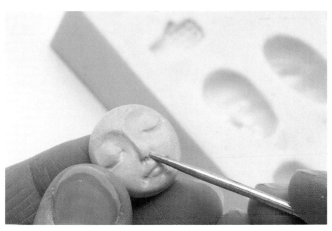

1 Oil the face mold with olive oil, using a brush to lightly coat. Roll a 1/2-inch ball of PMC, flatten the ball a bit, and press it into one of the face molds.

2 Use the knitting needle to gently define each nostril and shape the facial features if needed.

3 Repeat step 1 to mold one hand. Use the stir stick to make a hole in the hand for hanging.

4 Transfer the clay face to the marble and gently press it to conform to the rounded shape. Sit the marble on one of the small face molds to keep it from rolling as the clay dries.

5 Make another 1/2-inch ball of metal clay for the back of the head. Flatten the ball so it is similar in size and shape to the face mold. Oil the molding mat and press the clay into it to add texture. Put this piece on the marble next to the clay face to dry.

6 Make the polymer clay body while the silver clay pieces are drying. Condition a ball of polymer clay. Shape it into a desired shape (round or squared). Spray the Sculpey texture sheet with a mist of water and press the ball on the desired area of the texture sheet. The water will act as a release agent, resulting in a better impression.

7 Use the needle tool to make a hole that goes all the way through the bead.

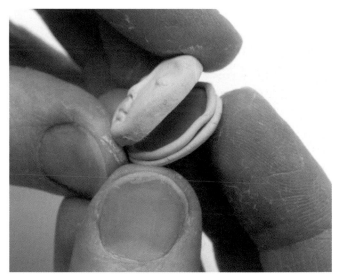

8 With your finger, gently rub Pearl-Ex powders on the textured area of the bead. (Wear a dust mask for safety while working with loose powders.) Bake the bead on a clean sheet of paper on a glass baking dish or tile at 275°F for 30 minutes. Let the piece cool in the oven.

9 When the head pieces are dry, dry fit the two halves together. Sand or carve away any high areas. Join the pieces by brushing water on the edges all around. Apply a line of syringe clay on one of the face halves. Press the two halves together and allow the piece to dry.

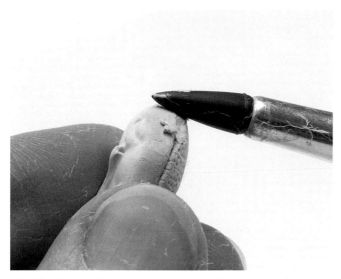

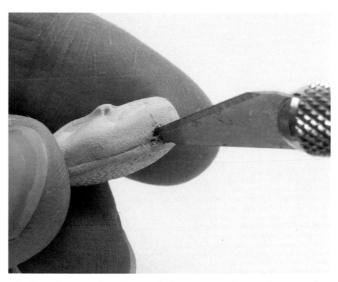

10 Fill the edges as needed using syringe clay or slip. Use a clay shaper to smooth the clay into the seams. Let the head dry thoroughly.

11 Using a craft knife, mark the center point on the top of the head and the chin, or bottom. Twirl the point of the knife to drill a hole at each end that is about 1/8 inch in diameter.

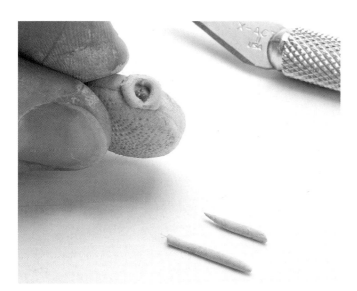

12 Roll two small snakes of clay. Position a snake over the rim of one hole, forming a circle. Cut the snake to fit and smooth the seam with water and a brush. Use some syringe clay to help attach the snakes. Repeat with the other hole.

Sand the sides of the head smooth with the nail file. Finish with 800-grit wet/dry sandpaper and polishing papers. Refine the hand, sanding as needed.

Place the dried face bead and the hand on a bed of vermiculite or a fiber blanket in the kiln. Fire at the temperatures recommended for PMC+. Burnish the metal clay with a brass brush to the desired finish.

13 Cut the sterling wire into four 9-inch pieces. Set one wire aside; this will be used for the arms later. Form the spiral hair, forming coils at the end of three of the wires. Use flat nose pliers to hold the wire as you coil it as shown in this photo.

15 Use the remaining wire to form the arms. Hold the center of the arm wire at the base of the head and wrap around a few times to create the neck.

14 Run the wires through the head so the spirals are on top. Bend into shape for the hairdo. Slide the polymer clay "body" bead onto the three wires.

16 String the glass beads on the arm and leg wires. (Notice that there is another wire between the legs; pull this extra wire aside.)

17 Make a spiral at the end of one arm, and a wire-wrapped loop on the other using round-nose pliers. You can attach the silver hand to this loop or use a jump ring to attach the hand to the loop if you want it to be a bit longer. Make wire-wrapped loops for the feet.

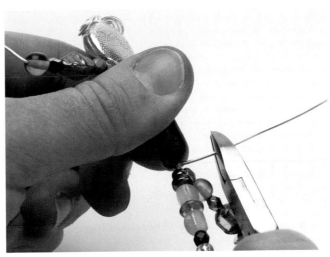

18 Clip off the extra wire you set aside in step 16, leaving about 1/2 inch.

19 Tuck the end of the wire up inside the polymer bead to hide the end.

20 Attach a pin back with a small strip of polymer clay, pressing the edges of the strip to the back of the doll body. Bake the entire piece again at 275°F for about 15 minutes. (The pin back can be glued on using superglue instead if desired.)

Crocheting with Beads & Charms

THERE ARE A VARIETY of fiber techniques you can incorporate into your metal clay designs. If you love needlework, combining metal with soft rich fibers is a fun and satisfying way to create jewelry pieces. Macramé, Chinese knotting, and tatting are a few examples of fiber techniques you can use for jewelry. In this project, silver clay elements, freshwater pearls, and faceted beads are crocheted along silk embroidery cord to create a soft flowing design.

TO MAKE ONE NECKLACE, YOU WILL NEED:

- Art Clay Silver Standard or 650/1200 Low Fire
- Basic metal clay supplies
- Two-part silicon rubber mold putty (Belicone®)
- Object to mold star-shaped ornament
- Cubic zirconia stones
- Textured seashell
- Silk embroidery cord (Kanagawa embroidery silk; Piecemakers or Lacis)
- Size 5 metal crochet hook
- Freshwater pearls
- AB crystal beads
- Seed beads
- Beading needle
- Purchased clasp (optional)

CROCHETED NECKLACE *by Sherri Haab*

1 For the centerpiece of this necklace a star shape was molded from a cast ornament. Knead equal parts of each component of the two-part silicone rubber putty until uniform in color.

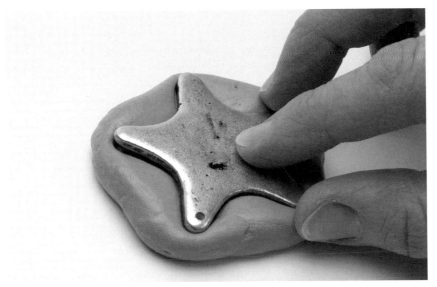

2 Form the putty into a ball and flatten on a smooth clean surface. Press the ornament face down into the putty, making sure the putty surrounds the ornament on all sides.

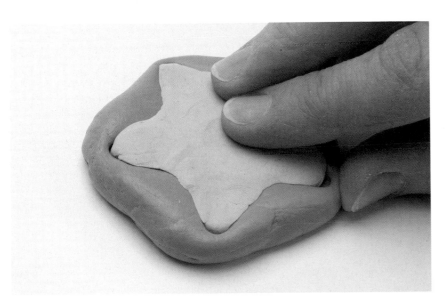

3 Let the putty set up with the ornament in place. You can tell when the putty has cured if you press on it with your fingernail and it bounces back without leaving an impression. This takes about 30 minutes or less. Remove the ornament. Press a ball of soft moist metal clay into the mold, smoothing the back of the clay to fill the edges of the mold. Remove excess clay as necessary.

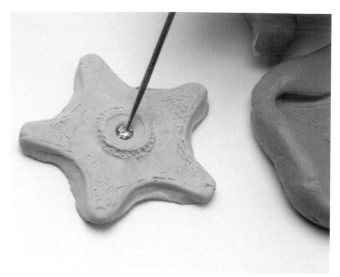

4 Turn the mold over and flex to release the clay onto a smooth flat surface. Use a needle tool to make a generous hole for hanging at one of the points. Push cubic zirconia stones into the clay until they are just below the surface of the clay. This will allow the clay to shrink in around the top edge of the stones as it fires, holding the stones in place.

5 If you have shallow areas where you can't push the stones below the level of the clay, add small ropes of clay to form "bezels" around the stones. Attach the ropes of clay with water and slip. When the piece is firm enough to hold its shape, repair cracked areas with a paintbrush and water. Set it aside to dry. Use a nail file to smooth the edges before firing.

6 Make organic-looking "sea shapes" for the beads that will decorate the necklace. For one element, I formed a rope of clay into a ring shape and then textured it with a seashell.

7 Other small bead shapes were formed by hand, using a needle tool to poke holes for stringing later. The clay was left very rough, with very little refinement other than sizing the holes before firing. None of these were formed around bead cores; they were left solid and slightly flattened.

Fire the star-shaped centerpiece and accent beads as directed for Art Clay Silver. Brass brush, polish, and finish the pieces as desired. Add a patina if you want to darken the textured areas.

8 Lay out the centerpiece and beads to form the pattern or order for the necklace. Alternate the silver clay beads with seed beads, faceted crystals, and freshwater pearls. String half of the necklace elements onto the end of the bead cord with a beading needle. (String the bead closest to the center of the necklace on first; the last bead added will be the bead that ends up near the clasp. I usually end with a series of about ten seed beads next to the clasp.)

9 Remove the beading needle and begin to make a chain stitch by forming a slip knot about 6 inches from the end of the cord. Insert the crochet hook into the slip knot, and pull tight.

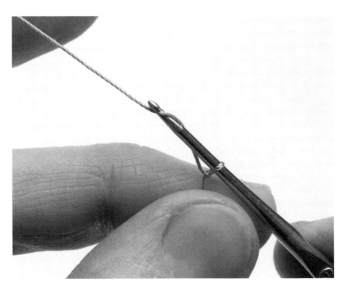

10 To make the first stitch, wrap the yarn over the hook as shown.

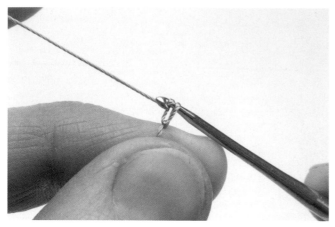

11 Catch the cord with the crochet hook and pull it through the slip knot.

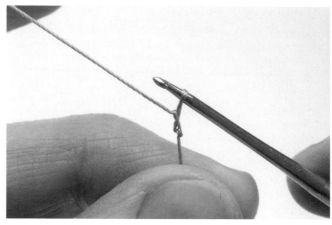

12 The cord you just pulled through the slip knot will now be on your hook, forming one chain stitch.

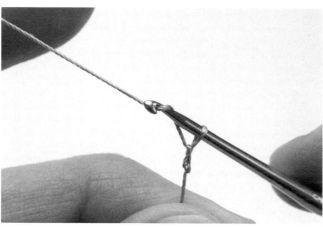

13 Make a few more chain stitches with the cord in the same way to get started.

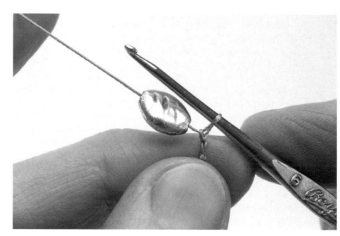

14 To begin crocheting beads along the chain, start with the last seed bead you added in step 8. (This photo shows a larger bead along the sequence for illustration purposes.) Slide this bead down to the hook.

15 Move the bead close to the last chain stitch you just made and catch the cord behind the bead.

16 Bring the cord through the chain stitch as shown. (All of the beads along the cord are crocheted into the chain in the same manner. You will notice that this chain stitch is intentionally longer to accomodate the length of the bead.)

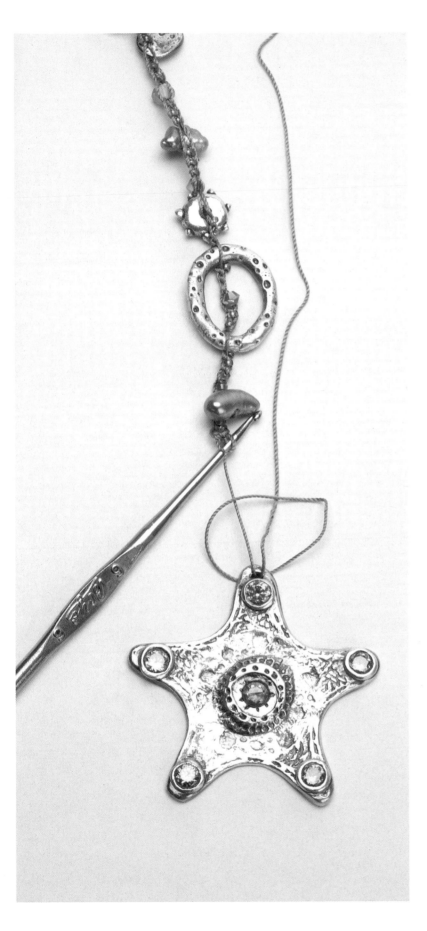

17 The silver "oval" shapes are crocheted into the design by catching one side, crocheting down the length inside the oval and then catching the other side to secure. To gauge the finished length of the necklace, measure occasionally until you have completed half of the desired length of the necklace. If you need to add a few beads, unwind a few yards of cord from the card and add them to that end with a beading needle. If you have too many beads, slide them down the cord to use for the other half or side of the necklace. At the midpoint, add the center piece by pinching the cord in half and passing it through the hole for hanging (this will make a loop). Pull the loop through the hole so that it is big enough to pass both cords (finished side and the unfinished cord) along with the hook through to form a lark's-head knot as shown. This photo shows the loop through the hole with the both sides of the necklace cord passed through the loop.

Slide the loop and pendant piece until they are as close to the completed side as possible. You will now be ready to continue crocheting a chain to form the other side.

Roll off a couple of yards of cord from the card, add a beading needle, and thread on beads to form the other side. I find it helpful to add only a few beads at a time to form a pleasing design to complement the first side. My design is asymmetrical, using beads to harmonize the completed side. Finish with a series of seed beads and a few chain stitches at the end, making sure both sides are even in length. Pull the end of the cord through the last loop to fasten off.

To complete the necklace, you can either tie on a purchased clasp or just leave the ends of the necklace long enough to tie. Tie extra beads on the ends of the cords for a decorative accent.

Creating Buttons, Clasps & Buckles

METAL CLAY affords the freedom to make one-of-a-kind buttons, toggles, and focal pieces to complement the jewelrymaking materials you are working with. In this project, vintage-style bracelets are made from antique ribbon and handmade silver components. For a professional look, you may prefer to line the back of the ribbon bracelets with Ultrasuede®. Sew a strip along the edge to the inside of the ribbon. This will give the bracelet form and body to hold its shape.

LOOP-AND-TOGGLE CLASP

For this bracelet I created a clasp by cutting the rolled clay freehand and left the edges rough for an organic look. Using antique ribbon adds to the charm of the bracelet.

TO MAKE ONE BRACELET, YOU WILL NEED:

- PMC+
- Basic metal clay supplies
- Fine silver casting grains (PMC Supply)
- Cubic zirconia stone
- Head pin
- Crystal bead
- Small length of chain
- Jump ring
- Ribbon (about 9 inches in length)
- Needle and thread or fabric glue

LOOP-AND-TOGGLE CLASP BRACELET *by Sherri Haab*

1 Roll out a sheet of clay, about ⅛ inch thick, to make the decorative loop. Cut out a shape with an open space in the middle (as wide as or a little wider than the ribbon). Texture the surface with a needle tool and add small ropes of clay, using water to attach. Push some silver grains into the clay to embed. Press a cubic zirconia into the clay and surround the top of the stone with a rope of clay. Blend all of the clay attachments with water and slip as needed.

Make a toggle with the same texture. The length of the toggle should be longer than the opening of the loop in every direction so that it won't slip through when you wear the bracelet.

2 Make another loop for the other end of the ribbon, with the opening being a little longer than the width of the ribbon. Use slip and a clay shaper to blend a small clay loop to the side of this piece. Pierce a hole in the center of the toggle piece with a needle tool. Let the pieces dry until bone dry. Sand and refine the edges if needed.

Fire the pieces as directed for PMC+ and finish the fired pieces with a brass brush, leaving a bright silver finish. Burnish the high spots with a burnishing tool.

3 To assemble the bracelet, start with the toggle. Thread a crystal bead on a head pin and then through the hole on the toggle. Make a wrapped loop at the end of the head pin to attach the toggle to a small length of chain. Attach the chain to the small metal clay loop with a jump ring. Thread one end of the ribbon through this small loop, and thread the other end of the ribbon through the large decorative loop as shown. Adjust the length of the ribbon to fit when the bracelet is clasped. Use a bit of fabric glue or a needle and thread to tack the ends of the ribbon down to the inside of the bracelet.

BUTTON CLASP

For this project, I made a mold of an antique button to create two silver button clasps. Small objects such as a doll face, an old brooch, or even a cheap plastic toy can also be cast and then transformed into silver buttons for a different look.

TO MAKE ONE BRACELET, YOU WILL NEED:

- Art Clay Silver Standard
- Basic metal clay supplies
- Two-part silicone rubber putty (Belicone)
- Button to cast

- Small piece of 20-gauge fine silver wire
- Wide ribbon (about 9 inches in length)
- Hem sealant
- Needle and thread
- Seed beads

BUTTON CLASP BRACELET *by Sherri Haab*

1 To make a mold of an existing button, mix a small ball of each component of the silicone rubber putty until uniform in color (see page 59). Press the button into the putty, making sure the sides are surrounded by the putty. Let it sit about 10 minutes until firm. Remove the button. The mold can now be used to make multiple buttons with metal clay. Roll a small ball of metal clay and press it into the mold until the back is level with the top of the mold. Clip off and bend a small piece of wire in half to make the button shank. Push it into the back of the clay.

2 Let the clay sit for about an hour; carefully flex the mold to release the clay button. (If the button is hard to remove, let it dry completely.) After removing, let the clay continue to dry. When the clay is bone dry, sand the edges with a nail file or sandpapers. Make the second button in the same fashion.

  Fire both buttons on a fiber blanket or vermiculite as directed for Art Clay Silver. Finish the pieces as desired.

  To make the bracelet, seal the cut ends of the ribbon with hem sealant. Fold one of the ends to the inside of the bracelet (about 1/2 inch). Stitch along the folded edge to attach it to the inside of the ribbon. Sew each of the buttons close to the edge of the ribbon on the front.

3 Measure and adjust the length of the bracelet to fit. Fold over the other edge of the ribbon and sew in place. Thread a needle with strong thread (doubled) and thread on enough seed beads to make a loop that will fit over and around the button. Sew back down into the ribbon to finish the loop, knot on the back side. Make a second loop for the other button.

BEADED BUCKLE

Fabric rolled across metal clay creates a soft texture, which complements the beaded stitching design used as a focal piece on this ribbon bracelet.

TO MAKE ONE BRACELET, YOU WILL NEED:

- Art Clay Silver Standard
- Basic metal clay supplies
- Syringe clay or thick slip
- Strip of cardboard or mat board
- Beads
- C-Lon® nylon bead cord (#18)

- Wax-melting tool or lighter
- Ribbon (about 9 inches in length)
- Button
- Seed beads
- Needle and thread

BEADED BUCKLE BRACELET *by Sherri Haab*

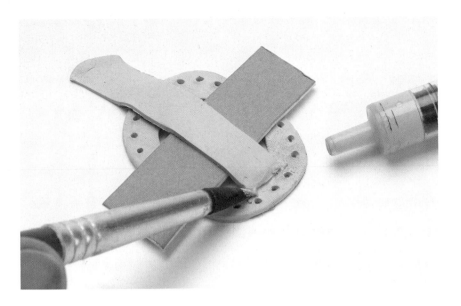

1 Roll out a sheet of clay, four cards thick. Texture the surface by rolling a piece of fabric over the clay. Cut out an oval shape for the buckle. To cut out the inside shape where the ribbon will pass through, measure the width of the ribbon to be used for the bracelet and add a little room for shrinkage. Use a needle tool to make holes around the edge of the oval. Let the piece dry until leather hard.

Add a strip of clay to the back side of the buckle to make a channel to hold the ribbon. Roll the clay out about three cards thick and cut a strip, draping it over a piece of cardboard to fit the length of the opening. Attach the ends of the strip with syringe clay or thick slip.

2 Let the piece dry and add another layer of syringe clay or slip to make the attachment extra strong. After the piece is bone dry, refine the edges by sanding and use the tip of a knife to enlarge the holes if necessary.

Fire the piece in a kiln with the cardboard in place at any of the temperatures recommended for Art Clay Silver. After firing the piece, finish with a brass brush and burnishing tools.

3 Starting from the back of the buckle, thread a length of cord (about 24 inches) through one of the holes. Leave a 4-inch tail of cord in the back. Add the beads one at a time and use a whipstitch to sew the beads around the edge as shown.

After sewing through the last hole, tie the ends of the cord in the back with a tight square knot, cut off the excess, and melt the ends of the cord with a wax-melting tool or lighter to seal. (You can use white glue to seal the knot instead.) Thread the ribbon through the buckle. Finish the ends of the ribbon as described above for the button-clasp bracelet.

Using Metal Clay as a Support or Bezel

In jewelrymaking, the term *bezel* usually refers to a ring or rim of metal that surrounds and holds a gem or stone in place, but it can also simply describe any form that is used to feature an object or material. With metal clay, you can easily sculpt a bezel in any shape you wish to showcase such diverse materials as polymer clay, resin, concrete, and collage images. Some materials, including certain stones or glass, can be fired along with the metal clay, while most need to be added after the piece is fired.

Resin

THERE ARE SEVERAL TYPES of resin used in jewelrymaking. The projects in this book use epoxy resin, which is widely available. Envirotex Lite®, Colores™, Devcon 2-Ton® or Devcon 5-Minute® are just a few brand names on the market. There are three subcategories of epoxy resin: adhesives, coating resins, and casting resins.

The first type can be found in the adhesives section of any hardware or craft store. The resin is a two-part system that is usually packaged in small dual-tube dispensers. The resin is mixed thoroughly and then left to cure overnight, although some quick-setting formulas take only minutes to cure. This type of epoxy is useful for small applications, such as gluing on a pin back.

Coating, or embedding, resin is bottled in larger containers than the adhesive type and is sold in craft and hobby stores. Because it is formulated as a pouring resin, it is often less viscous and usually cures slower than an epoxy resin adhesive. Coating resin is durable and self-leveling, creating a smooth, clear, glass-like surface when dry.

Casting resin is a similar product but it allows you to pour deeper layers than coating resin. Both coating and casting types of epoxy resin come in two parts (resin and hardener) that are mixed thoroughly.

Fired metal clay and epoxy resin can be used together in many exciting ways. Clear resin looks like glass and can be used protect pictures or small collage elements in a bezel. Applying the resin and collage elements in layers creates depth in a piece of jewelry. Some artists fill recessed areas in silver with pigmented or dyed resins to simulate glass enamel. Pigment powders, glitter, gold leaf, paper images, and other small objects can all be embedded in epoxy resin.

It is important to mix and cure resin properly. Resin and hardener must be mixed thoroughly for proper curing. Always transfer the resin to a second cup and mix it again before applying, to ensure success. Resin cures better in warm temperatures. Place the resin under a lightbulb or in a warm area to facilitate curing.

Air bubbles are a common problem with resin. Passing a heat gun (the type used for melting embossing powders for rubber stamping; not a hair dryer) over the uncured resin will generate heat and get rid of most of the bubbles.

You should always wear a respirator, rubber gloves, and eye protection when you work with resin. Resin can cause skin sensitivity, and although newer formulations of resin are low-odor, they still produce fumes that are harmful to breathe. Follow all manufacturers' safety guidelines carefully.

FAUX DICHROIC GLASS PENDANT *by Jacqueline Lee* Jacqueline filled a metal clay bezel with layers of polymer clay, glitter, powdered pigments, and epoxy resin to simulate the shimmer of dichroic glass.

LEFT: ROCK CHERUB *by Robert Dancik* This charming brooch combines PMC, paper pulp, sterling silver, copper, and epoxy resin. (Photo by Douglas Foulke.)

OPPOSITE: CHARM BRACELET *by Wendy Wallin Malinow and Sherri Haab* Colored resin can be painted on fired metal clay to simulate the look of enamel. This bracelet made of PMC, polymer clay, and resin is a variation on the project on page 115.

Constructing a Ring with a Deep Bezel

METAL CLAY can be sculpted in (almost) any shape imaginable to create a unique setting for unusual materials. This three-dimensional design by Wendy Wallin Malinow features polymer clay, resin, and colorful beads set in a silver, bell-shaped flower. It's a bouquet you can wear on your finger and it doesn't even need to be watered!

TO MAKE ONE RING, YOU WILL NEED:

- PMC3
- Basic metal clay supplies
- Cork clay
- Sobo® glue
- Ring mandrel
- Teflon paper or HattieS™ ring-forming strip
- HattieS™ Patties™ ring forms
- Polymer clay
- Head pins
- Crystal beads
- Crimp beads
- Epoxy resin (Envirotex Lite)
- Mixing cups and stick for resin
- Glitter (optional)
- Aluminum foil
- Heat gun (optional)

FLOWER RING *by Wendy Wallin Malinow*

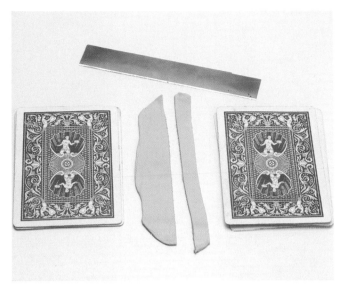

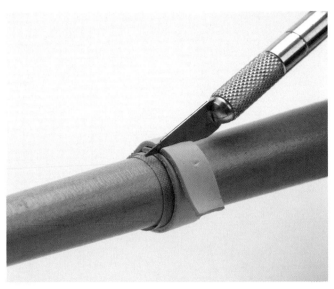

1 Make a 3/8-inch ball of cork clay to form the flower shape. Let the ball dry and coat with a layer of Sobo glue. To prepare the mandrel, you will need a strip of Teflon paper or a ring-forming strip that is two sizes bigger than the finished ring. Cut the strip a little longer than this to overlap, and secure with tape. (A mandrel with ring sizes marked helps to get an accurate measurement.) Put the taped strip on the mandrel.

To make the ring band, roll out a sheet of PMC3, three cards thick. Cut a strip of clay about 3/8 inch wide and a little longer than the taped strip on the mandrel.

2 Wrap the clay loosely around the strip on the mandrel, over-lapping the clay. Use a knife or blade to cut through both layers at an angle. Remove the excess clay.

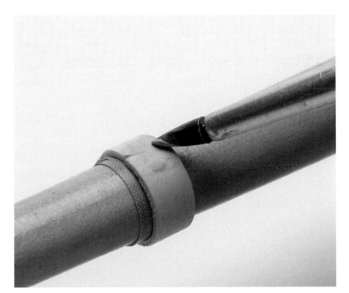

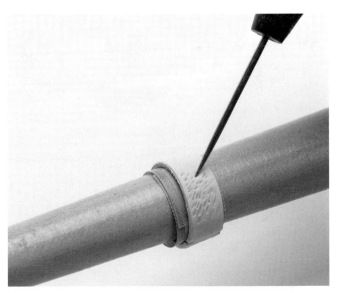

3 Use a clay shaper to blend the seam in the ring band with a little water or slip.

4 Add texture to the band with a needle tool if desired. Let the ring dry on the mandrel while you make the bezel.

5 Roll out a circle of clay about 1⅛ inches in diameter and about ¹⁄₁₆ inch thick. Cut out a flower shape with a knife.

6 Wrap the flower shape around the cork ball to form a cup. Add texture to the flower cup with a needle tool and let dry.

7 Attach the flower cup to the ring band on top of the seam with a generous amount of syringe clay, and smooth with a clay shaper to secure.

8 Let the ring continue to dry until firm enough to handle. Gently remove the ring from the mandrel and remove the strip from inside the ring. Let the ring dry completely. Check the seam and joints for cracks, and repair with syringe clay as needed. Sand the dried ring with a small sanding stick or sandpapers, softening the edges to make the ring more comfortable to wear.

To fire the ring, place a HattieS Patties form in the center of the ring. This will keep the ring from shrinking beyond the size you intend. Place the ring on a fiber blanket to keep it level. Fire in a kiln at 1472°F for 30 minutes with a slow ramp speed of 1500°F per hour (this is the temperature and time required for firing cork clay). After the ring is cooled, remove the form with water and a needle tool according to the manufacturer's instructions. Brass brush and burnish the silver, and add a patina to darken the recessed textures.

9 Coat the inside of the flower with a thin layer of glue. Let it dry until tacky. Line the inside of the flower with a small bit of polymer clay.

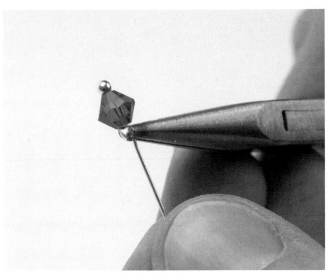

10 To make the flowers, thread crystal beads onto head pins. Use pliers to smash a crimp bead under each bead; this will help hold the beads in place.

11 Clip the head pins to a desired length and stick them into the clay before baking. Bake the ring at 275°F for 20 minutes to cure the polymer clay. Let the ring cool in the oven.

12 Prop the ring up with aluminum foil before filling with resin. Mix up a small amount of resin to fill the flower cup. Use a toothpick to add the resin to the inside of the flower, being careful not to overfill. If any air bubbles remain after a few minutes, run a heat gun over the resin, holding it about 10 inches above the ring. Allow the resin to cure at least overnight or for several days in a warm place (at least 75°F).

Embedding Collage Elements in Resin

ARTIST WENDY WALLIN MALINOW layered colorful bits of polymer clay, rhinestones, glitter, and old photos with resin in hollow silver bezels to make these intriguing charms. Make sure the items you embed in the resin are free of moisture and oil; dyed objects in particular might bleed or react with the resin. Adding the collage elements in layers, and letting the resin set up in between layers, adds dimensional interest to the bezels.

TO MAKE ONE BRACELET, YOU WILL NEED:

- PMC3
- Basic metal clay supplies
- Cork clay
- Sobo glue
- Paper images
- Decoupage glue (Mod Podge®)
- Small brush for glue
- Small amounts of polymer clay in various colors
- Rhinestones
- Glitter, beads, or other small inclusions
- Epoxy casting resin (EasyCast®)
- Mixing cup and stick for resin
- Heat gun (optional)
- Head pins
- Chain for toggle (a few inches long)

COLLAGE CUPS BRACELET *by Wendy Wallin Malinow*
The collage cups in this photo were textured with a stamping tool, and little balls of clay were attached to add dimension. The following steps show how you can use an ordinary ballpoint pen to create your own playful dot pattern.

1 The cups, the connections, and the clasp all contribute to the length of the bracelet; keep this in mind as you plan your design. This bracelet was made with seven cups ranging from ½ inch to 1 inch wide. Begin by rolling cork clay into shapes on which to form the clay bezels. Flatten them slightly so that the bezels will be about ¼ inch deep. Let the cork forms dry and coat with a layer of Sobo glue, letting it dry until tacky.

To make a bezel, roll out a piece of clay about five cards thick. Shape the clay around the cork form to create a cup shape. Trim around the top so that the sides of the cup are even.

2 Make as many bezels as you would like to include in your bracelet. Texture the clay as desired. The top of a ballpoint pen makes a fun texture.

3 Pierce a small hole in each side of the bezels with a needle tool. These holes will be used for connecting head pins; each hole should be just big enough for the head pin to pass through. Place the hole at the midpoint of the wall height.

4 To make a loop-and-toggle clasp, roll out a piece of clay about ⅛ inch thick and cut out a square. Two square cutters can be used, or you can cut the shape freehand.

5 Texture the clay in the same way as the bezel cups and pierce a hole on one side. Form a toggle for the clasp by rolling a log of clay and tapering the ends. Make the toggle longer than the opening of the square. Pierce the toggle in the center with a needle tool.

6 Let the bezel cups and loop-and-toggle clasp pieces dry thoroughly. Sand and make repairs as needed; the edges of the bezel cups should be as even as possible. Place the pieces on a bed of alumina hydrate, vermiculite, or a fiber blanket and fire in a kiln at 1472°F for 30 minutes with a slow ramp speed 1500°F per hour (this is the temperature and time required for firing cork clay).

After the pieces are cool, brass brush and burnish the silver and add a patina. Buff the surface, leaving the recessed areas dark.

Insert a head pin through each hole in the bezels, with the head of the pin on the inside. Use a needle tool to widen the holes if needed, but just enough for the head pin to fit.

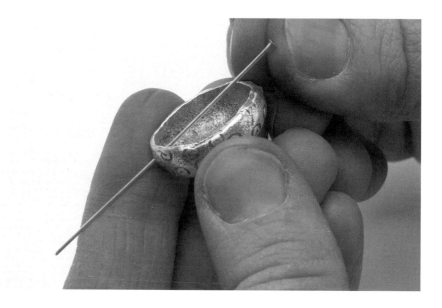

7 Decide which inclusions you want to put in the bezel cups. Coat images on both sides with decoupage glue to keep them from "bleeding" in the resin. Let them dry. Line the inside of the cups with polymer clay as a base.

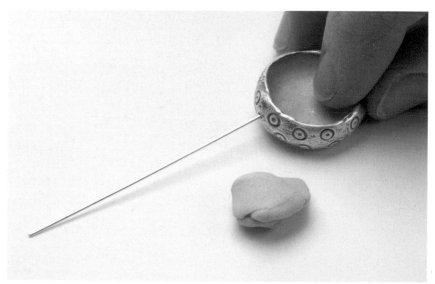

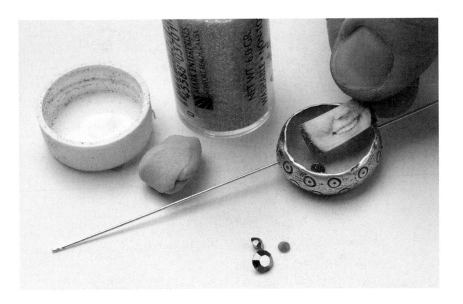

8 Add the inclusions, pushing rhinestones, beads, and images into the surface of the clay. Sprinkle glitter and/or bits of polymer clay into the cups if desired. Bake the cups in an oven at 275°F for 30 minutes to cure the polymer clay. Let the cups cool in the oven.

9 Mix the epoxy casting resin thoroughly and use a craft stick to fill the cups with resin.

Release air bubbles from the resin by holding a heat gun about 10 inches above the resin and passing it back and forth. Let the cups set in a warm place (at least 75°F) overnight or for several days until cured.

10 Arrange the cups and the loop-and-toggle clasp components in the desired order to form the bracelet. Make loops with the head pins to connect the cups. The loops should be perpendicular to each other (one vertical, the next horizontal). Connect the loops and wrap the ends of the wires close to the bezel cups. Clip off the excess wire.

Glass & Ceramics

ONE OF THE MOST exciting aspects of working with metal clay is the ability to fire it with materials such as glass and ceramics. PMC3 and Art Clay Silver 650/1200 Low Fire metal clays work especially well with glass and ceramics because they fire at lower temperatures than the other types of metal clay. It is important to understand the properties of these materials so that you will be successful in all of your projects that incorporate them.

All glass is sensitive to heat. If glass is heated or cooled too quickly it will crack. The kiln must be ramped at a rate that allows the glass to adjust to the heat. After firing the piece, the glass must be cooled slowly to prevent thermal shock. This can be accomplished by leaving the kiln door shut until the glass piece has cooled completely. Heating and cooling the glass properly to stabilize it and prevent strain is called *annealing*.

Annealing temperatures and lengths of time are determined by the type of glass used, and by the thickness of the glass. Larger pieces need to be annealed for longer periods of time. Refer to annealing charts provided by glass manufacturers for proper annealing temperatures and time recommendations for the type of glass used in a project.

Dichroic glass cabochons are a great choice for metal clay. Dichroic glass has a surface layer consisting of fine metal particles. The surface color has an iridescent quality that will vary depending on the angle at which you view it. Gem-like cabochons are made by fusing together and annealing layers of dichroic glass. Dichroic glass cabochons made with Bullseye or Uroboros glass can easily be fired with silver metal clay, because the temperatures used for the glass are compatible with low-firing metal clays.

NOT JUST A
CLAY HEART
by Karen L. Cohen
Cloisonné enamel in a PMC heart. The abstract design was created by combining fine silver wires, silver granulation balls, and gold foil with transparent leaded vitreous enamels.

Firing metal clay with ceramics and porcelain requires similar precautions as when firing with glass. Fire pottery shards at low temperatures and leave the kiln door closed until the pieces cool completely. Some glazes may change color when fired, so it's helpful to test-fire a piece when in doubt.

Enameling is the fusion of powdered glass to metal. Fired and burnished silver clay is ideal for enameling, because it is fine silver. Glass enamels can be applied to finished metal clay pieces, then fired and finished using the same techniques that you would use for traditional enameling. Enameling is beyond the scope of this book, but there are many books on the subject, such as *The Art of Fine Enameling* by Karen L. Cohen, who uses these techniques and incorporates metal clay into her fine enameling work.

ABOVE: DICHROIC GLASS RING *by Hattie Sanderson* PMC3, a dichroic glass cabochon, and a trillion-cut lab-grown gemstone combine to form this one-of-a kind ring. (Photo by the artist.)

LEFT: TRAVEL PIN *by Patti Leota Genack* A pottery shard was encased in PMC to create this fanciful pin.

Firing Silver with Dichroic Glass

DICHROIC GLASS is perfect for combining with metal clay. You can purchase dichroic glass cabochons, which are easy to work with and the just the right size for a pendant. Before firing, clean the cabochon with a cotton swab dipped in clear water to remove oil and residue. This will help prevent a haze from forming on the surface. Remember to ramp the heat up slowly and let the piece cool in the kiln.

TO MAKE ONE PENDANT, YOU WILL NEED:

- PMC3
- Syringe clay or thick slip
- Basic metal clay supplies
- Dichroic glass cabochon
- Leather-stamping tool for texture (optional)
- RapidPlater™ 24K Gold Plating Pen Kit (PMC Supply)

DICHROIC GLASS PENDANT *by Sherri Haab*
A beaded cord complements the colors in the dichroic glass. You can also add a dangle with beads and head pins if desired.

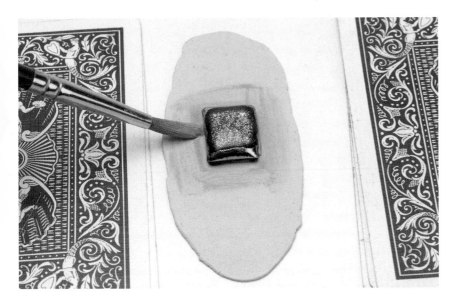

1 Roll out a sheet of clay three cards thick. Attach the cabochon to the clay with thick slip. Use a paintbrush dipped in water to keep the sheet of clay damp as you work on the bezel for the next step.

2 Roll out a long strip of clay using two strips of mat board as guides. Cut a narrow strip of clay about 3/16 inch wide (this will be the height of the bezel) and long enough to wrap loosely around the cabochon. Wrap the strip around the cabochon using slip to attach it to the clay base. (The strip will shrink around the cabochon, so it is important to wrap loosely.) Cut the ends of the strip to meet in a butt joint and blend the seam with a clay shaper. Trim the edges of the base into a rectangle shape; reserve the extra clay, keeping it moist and wrapped.

3 Add a ball of clay at each corner, attaching them with slip to the base sheet. Press a textured design onto the balls with a leather-stamping tool if desired.

4 Roll thin ropes of clay to make loops for hanging and attach to the top and bottom of the pendant using syringe clay or thick slip. Use a tool to blend the seams to the pendant. Add smaller balls of clay around the bezel for decoration, attaching each with slip. (Four small balls were attached on top of the textured corner balls created in step 3.)

5 Let the piece dry flat. Refine any cracks and smooth the seams with thick slip or moist clay. Smooth with a damp brush or a clay shaper.

When the piece is dry, file and sand the edges to refine. Use a clean brush with water to clean the surface of the cabochon. It is important not to touch the cabochon and to keep it free of oil or dirt, as this will leave a film after firing. Let the piece dry.

6 Note: These directions are for a small to medium-size cabochon, about 1/3 inch thick. Remember, do *not* fire glass with a torch, as it might shatter, sending glass pieces flying. Set the ramp speed of the kiln to 1500°F per hour and fire the piece at 1290°F for 10 minutes. Turn off the kiln at this point and let the piece cool completely with the door shut, usually overnight. The firing plus retained heat during cooling should be sufficient to anneal a small cabochon. For large cabochons, a longer annealing time may be required; refer to tables and charts from glass

manufacturers for more information. After the piece is cooled, brass brush and burnish until the desired finish is achieved.

Use a pen plater dipped in 24-karat gold solution to highlight the raised dots on the bezel. Follow the manufacturer's instructions and make sure the pen is well saturated. Attach the alligator clip to the piece as close to the area you wish to plate as possible. Apply the solution to the area; repeat for a darker gold.

Complete the necklace by hanging the pendant from a beaded cord.

Firing Silver with Ceramics

FOR THOUSANDS OF YEARS Asian artisans repaired cracked and broken ceramic objects using a natural lacquer the Japanese call *urushi*. Instead of trying to match the color of the lacquer to the original material, a coating of 23-karat gold was added to emphasize the contrast. By joining a ceramic shard and porcelain cabochon with metal clay, this project by artist Lora Hart pays homage to that ancient technique.

TO MAKE ONE PENDANT, YOU WILL NEED:

- PMC3
- PMC3 syringe clay and paste/slip
- Basic metal clay supplies
- Patterned brass texture plate(s)
- Ceramic shard
- "Moon Baby" cabochon (Earthenwood Studio)
- ½-inch circle template or circle cutter
- 2mm cubic zirconia or lab-grown gem (optional)
- Plastic drinking straw

URUSHI GODDESS PENDANT *by Lora Hart*
The woody texture of the goddess figure's "arms" is a subtle reference to the tree sap that is used to create *urushi* lacquer.

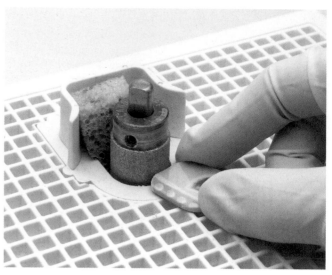

1 Prepare the ceramic shard before starting the project. If you do not have a ceramic shard, you can buy an inexpensive piece of china or other ceramic item at a thrift store and break it into pieces by placing it in a plastic bag wrapped with a dish towel and whacking at it with a hammer. The unique shapes that are formed by this method can bring unexpected visual movement to the final form. However, you can customize a shard using a ceramic tile nipper or cutter.

2 Gently round any sharp points on the shard with a metal file. Sharp points on the shards may stress the metal clay as it shrinks, forming a crack or break. Another option is to use a glass grinder made for stained glass. If you have access to one, it can make the job of rounding the shards much easier. This photo shows a glass grinder being used on the shard. Be sure to wear protective glasses and a dust mask while grinding. A rubber glove will help you to hold the shard and protects your fingers from the edges.

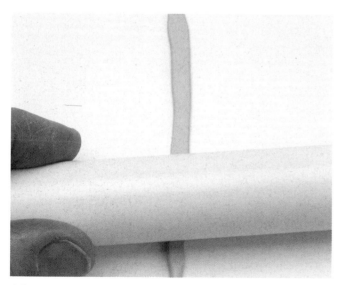

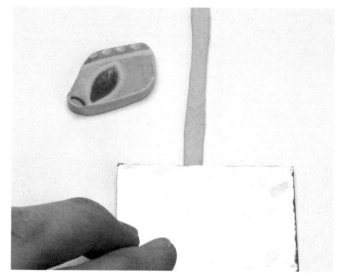

3 To create a bezel that will surround the shard, roll a rope of clay to a diameter of approximately 2¹/₂ to 3 mm, about the size of a large cocktail straw. Use a roller to flatten the coil slightly.

4 Press your texture on top with gentle pressure until you have a strip of clay that is about 2 mm wider than the thickest part of the shard. (The strip should not be thinner than about four playing cards thick.)

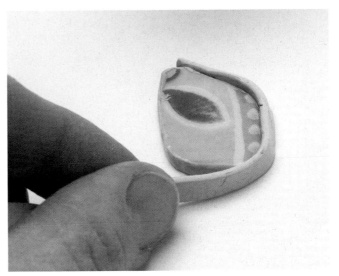

5 Moisten the underside of the strip and cover with a piece of plastic wrap to keep the strip fresh while you apply a layer of slip around the edge of the shard to attach the clay. If the shard has a nice finished edge (like the edge of a plate), you may chose to leave this area exposed and not wrap all the way around, so don't apply any slip to that area.

6 Loosely wrap the strip of clay around the shard, textured side out. Keep the edge centered with the strip extending about 1 mm on either side of the shard. Overlap the ends. Cut through the overlapped ends with a knife, remove the excess clay, and join the seam with a bit of water. It's a good idea to place the seam at the top of the shard where the arms will be placed. Set the shard aside to dry.

7 To make the back of the bezel setting for the cabochon, roll a sheet of clay three cards thick. Pick up the sheet and lay it on top of a texture plate with two playing cards on either side. Roll over it again to pick up the texture.

8 Cut a disk the exact size of the $1/2$-inch cabochon using a circle template or cutter and set aside to dry.

9 Apply a generous amount of thick slip to the untextured side of the disk and settle the cabochon on top of it. Make sure that there are no gaps underneath the cabochon by wiggling it a bit before centering it on the disk. Set aside to dry. Shape the dry disk with an emery board so it matches the circumference of the cabochon.

10 Prepare a strip of clay to create a bezel for the cabochon. (This strip of clay does not need to be as wide as the shard bezel because the face cabochon may not be as thick as the shard.)

11 Wrap the strip of clay around the cabochon using slip to adhere. Working on a flat surface will help ensure that the edge of the strip is flush with the clay disk backing the cabochon. Place the seam at the chin of the face so it will be hidden when all the parts are assembled. Set the head aside to dry.

12 Create five or six tiny decorative balls of clay. These do not have to be of a uniform size or shape. If desired, set a 2mm lab-grown gem by pressing it into a 4mm ball of clay, making sure to capture the girdle of the stone. The table (the largest facet on top of the stone) should be slightly below the surface of the clay to ensure a secure setting. Set these aside to dry.

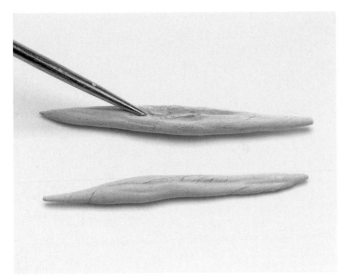

13 Form the arms by rolling two thicker coils approximately 1¼ to 1½ inches long. Since these will be replicating tree branches, use your fingers to create a slightly irregular shape and taper the ends a bit. Make subtle bends in the coil (tree limbs aren't straight) and let them air dry for 5 to 7 minutes. Use a needle tool to score a bark-like texture into the surface. Allow the little "crumbs" that develop as you scratch to remain. These add to the organic look and feel of the tree bark texture. Let these pieces dry completely.

14 Fit the arms together, one crossing over the other, and join with thick slip. If they don't nestle into each other naturally, use sandpaper or a file to create flat areas on the center of each and join them there. Set the pieces aside to dry again.

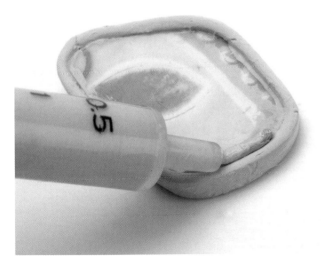

15 Before assembling the figure, fill seams and gaps around the shard and head where the metal clay and ceramic meet to ensure that the clay won't pull away from the sides as it shrinks during firing. Dampen the seam with water and apply a line of clay with the syringe. Pat the clay into the void with a barely damp paintbrush and use the brush or a clay shaper to smooth it, filling the gap. Follow the same directions to repair areas on the shard where the glaze has chipped away, or anywhere you want to leave the silver intentionally.

16 Metal clay will bond to the glaze, so be sure to thoroughly remove any dry clay residue with a wooden toothpick where it isn't wanted, then clean the ceramic piece thoroughly with a clean paintbrush dampened with water.

Sand the edges gently with fine-grit sandpaper as needed before moving on to the next step.

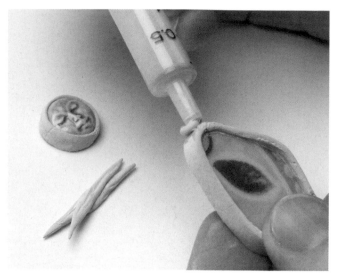

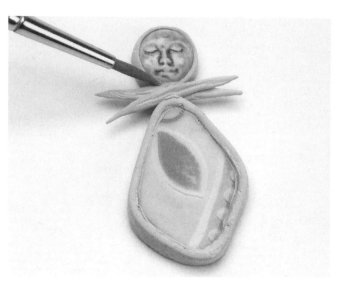

17 To assemble the figure, dampen the top of the ceramic shard's bezel and the bottom of the twiggy arms with a paintbrush, extrude a generous blob of syringe clay on the top of the bezel, press the two pieces together, and let dry.

18 Repeat step 17 to join the head to the top of the arms. Let the figure dry, then fill any gaps around the joints with syringe or slip for strength.

19 Finally, use a pair of tweezers to dip the little balls in thick slip and fit them into the crevices of the arms. The balls will stay in place better if you have at least three points of contact. Push the balls with tweezers or the tip of a needle tool to adhere tightly to the slip. Add the optional gem in the same way.

20 Make a bail for the back of the pendant by trimming a drinking straw to 1 inch in length and then cutting it in half to create a tunnel shape. Lubricate the rounded side of one piece with Badger Balm or olive oil to prevent the clay from sticking. Roll and texture a sheet of clay three cards thick and cut it into a strip about 1/4 inch wide. Bevel one end of the strip to reduce the thickness; this will help the strip to blend at the seam. Use slip to join this end to the top of the bezel at the back of the head. Place the oiled half straw across the back of the head and drape the strip over it, cutting the strip to fit, and cutting at an angle to bevel the strip at the seam. Join the piece to the back of the arms with more slip. The high arch in the bail will flatten slightly during firing as it shrinks.

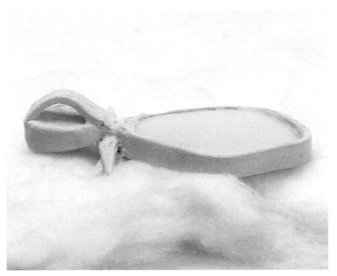

21 Let the bail dry, remove the straw, and reinforce the joint by adding "fillets" of syringe clay on the inside of the bail where it meets the back of the bezel cup. Smooth the syringe clay into the join with a paintbrush, let dry, and sand. Make sure to clean all ceramic surfaces.

22 Place the figure face down on a piece of ceramic fiber blanket in the kiln and fire at 1200°F for 45 minutes, using a slow ramp speed of 1500°F per hour. When the firing is done, leave the piece in the kiln to cool slowly. Do *not* open the door, even for a second! If you do, the glaze will craze. Remove the pendant only after the kiln has cooled down to 200°F or less.

23 Use a brass brush to burnish the silver to a soft sheen and tumble if desired. Due to the porosity of the material, ceramic pieces should be tumbled for a maximum of one hour at a time, letting the piece dry thoroughly between tumbling sessions. This piece was beautifully burnished after only 20 minutes.

24 If desired, you can use slip to sign the back of the shard with a maker's mark before firing. (This photo shows Lora's mark on the back of a finished piece.)

Filling a Bezel with Concrete

CONCRETE, a mixture of cement powders and aggregate mixed with water or acrylic add-mix, is an unusual material for jewelrymaking. Just try explaining to the guy at the hardware store what you need the concrete for. Wet concrete can be added to metal clay bezels and forms. It is a bit finicky to mix. You must have the correct proportion of water or add-mix for the concrete to set up with the proper strength. For best results, mix the concrete a bit dry. Robert Dancik designed this concrete and metal clay pendant.

TO MAKE ONE PENDANT, YOU WILL NEED:

- PMC Standard
- Basic metal clay supplies
- Texturing tool or surface
- Cubic zirconia stone or other stone suitable for firing (optional)
- Concrete (patching concrete such as Por-Rok®)
- Inclusions such as fired pieces of PMC, pearls, stones, etc.
- Large circle cutter or template
- Small square or other shape cutter
- Drinking straw or other cylindrical object to form tube
- Pallet knife or plastic knife
- Clear plastic cup for mixing concrete
- Acrylic grout additive or concrete add-mix
- Masking tape
- Purchased chain or cord for finished pendant

NOTE: Make thick and thin slip from PMC Standard to use in this project before beginning.

CONCRETE PENDANT
by Robert Dancik
Robert is a talented artist who makes beautiful pieces that combine fine metals with materials you might find in a hardware store. The contrast of a single pearl nestled in a bed of gray concrete creates a visual surprise.

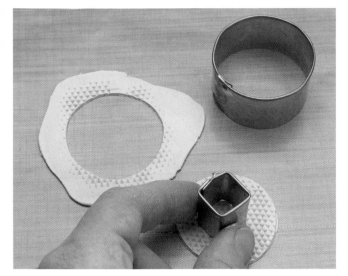

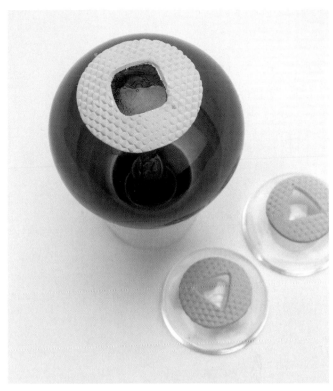

1 Roll out a thick (2mm) sheet of standard PMC, which is about the thickness of mat board. Texture one side of the sheet with a pattern by pressing a tool or textured surface onto the clay. This texture was created using a reflector.

Cut a 1½- to 2-inch circle from the sheet using a circle cutter or template (a cookie cutter can also be used). Keep in mind while choosing the size cutter to use that the clay will shrink about 25 percent. Cut a shape from the inside of the large circle to form a donut shape. A small square cutter was used in this piece, but you can use any shape you desire.

2 Drape the donut shape over a lightbulb or other domed surface and allow it to dry. (The smaller shapes in the photo are examples of different shapes you can cut out of the circle.)

3 When the clay is dry, sand the edges lightly on the outside and inside of the donut, using a nail file or sandpaper. The donut is extremely fragile at this stage; be very careful not to break the piece.

4 Roll a coil about ⅛ inch in diameter and about 4 inches long, and form it into a circle. The circle coil should fit about half way up the inside of the donut. Coat one "side" of the coil and the inside of the donut with slip and join the coil to the donut, forming a raised circle inside the donut. This coil will just be used to create a mechanical bond to hold the clay in place, so it doesn't need to be neat.

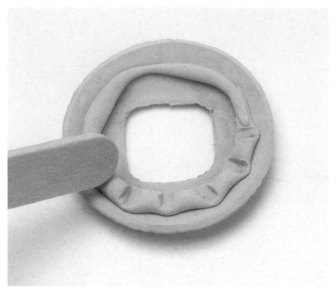

5 While the clay is still soft, press a craft stick into the coil at an angle to form open slits all around the circle. This ring will act as an anchor for the concrete and "lock" it into place.

6 Roll out another sheet of clay to form the bail for the top. Texture the sheet as desired. Cut a long triangle, 1½ to 2 inches long and about 1 inch wide at one end.

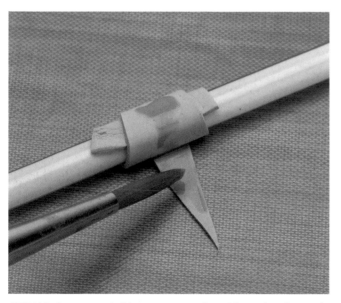

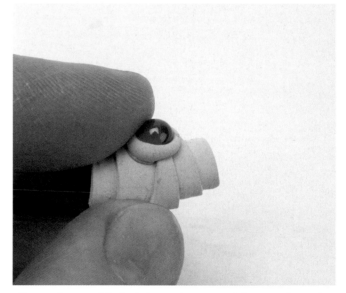

7 With the textured side out, start at the wide end and wrap it around a thick drinking straw. As you wrap, paint the overlapping section with thin slip to seal it. Allow the bail to dry and slide it off the straw.

8 Attach a small ball of clay to the point of the triangle on the bail with a bit of thick slip. Press the stone into the ball until it is just below the surface. Neaten the joint of the ball and the bail as needed with a paintbrush and allow the piece to dry.

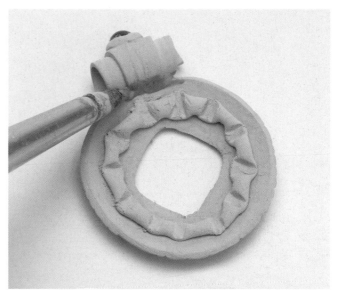

9 Decide which point of the donut pendant you want to be the top when it is hanging. With a sanding stick or file, make a small, flat area on the top edge of the donut and the bottom of the bail, so that there will be a similar size flat area on each.

10 Apply slip to both flat spots and join them firmly. Clean up any extra slip and neaten the joint.

11 Fire the pieces at 1650°F for 2 hours. Brass brush, burnish, and oxidize the piece to add a patina. Buff with sandpapers, leaving the recessed areas dark. Make sure to burnish the edge of the disk well, as this will make it easier to remove any concrete that may stick to it later.

12 Decide which inclusion will go in the center cutout, this example uses a small turquoise nugget. Place a piece of masking tape over the cutout with the sticky side facing the inside of the disk. Place the inclusion face down on the tape and press to make sure it is held firmly.

13 Place about 2 or 3 tablespoons of concrete powder in a small, clear plastic cup and add about 2 teaspoons of grout additive or water. Mix thoroughly with a disposable knife or craft stick, making sure there are no dry spots (look at the sides and bottom through the clear cup to check the mixture). The mixture should be fairly stiff and crumbly. Add more liquid a few drops at a time and incorporate completely before adding more. The mixture should be about the consistency of stiff, sandy whipped cream with a slightly shiny surface. There should not be a layer of water on top. If you add too much liquid, mix in just a little dry concrete and stir very thoroughly.

14 Using a pallet knife or similar utensil, scoop a bit of concrete mixture into the inside of the disk. Push the concrete around the turquoise with a toothpick or small craft stick to make sure it is surrounded. Fill about one-third of the disk and tap around the edge and from underneath the disk to level out the concrete. Put in more concrete and repeat until the disk "cup" is almost full. Each time you tap to level the concrete you will find that it looks rather wet on top; this is normal and will not have an adverse effect. Continue to add concrete to form a dome.

15 Place the pearl on the concrete dome and wiggle it back and forth to settle it. With a cotton swab or soft cloth, wipe off any concrete that may have gotten onto the disk or the inclusions. Put the piece aside to set for about 10 minutes. With a soft, small paintbrush, brush the top of the concrete very gently to even out the surface and to impart a bit of texture, if desired.

After about an hour, gently peel off the tape and brush the concrete inside the cutout and around the inclusion. At this point it is important for the concrete to cure (achieve full hardness). Depending on the thickness of the concrete and the ambient humidity, this may take two to three days. Put the piece in a warm place (no warmer than 175°F) to hasten drying. When the piece is no longer cool to the touch and has turned a light gray, it is cured. At this point, you can grind, sand, or file the concrete.

If there is any haze left on the piece from the concrete slurry, it can be removed with a cotton swab, a soft cloth, or just by rubbing with your finger. Add a chain or cord to finish the pendant.

Working with Colored Cement

WHO SAYS CEMENT has to be gray? You can add color to cement and concrete to produce a variety of exciting hues. There are a few things to keep in mind when coloring cement. Because cement is alkaline, it may cause some ordinary pigments to break down, so use pigments and dyes that are specifically made for grout or cement. Be sure to read all of the manufacturer's instructions for use. Remember that liquid pigments will add moisture to the mix, and be careful not to add too much. This project uses a white cement sculpting mixture. Because the mixture is white, the colors come through brighter than they would in gray cement or concrete.

TO MAKE ONE RING, YOU WILL NEED:

- Art Clay Silver Slow Dry
- Basic metal clay supplies
- Ring mandrel
- Teflon paper or HattieS ring-forming strip
- HattieS Patties Ring form
- Disposable cup and plastic knife

- Winterstone® Sculpting Stone white sculpting mixture (The Compleat Sculptor)
- Mixol® tinting paste (The Compleat Sculptor)
- Toothpick
- Plastic bag

HIS AND HERS RINGS *by Sherri Haab*

The steps that follow describe how to make the "his" ring (left). The "hers" ring was created in a similar way, but the bezel was formed as a separate piece and then attached to a ring base.

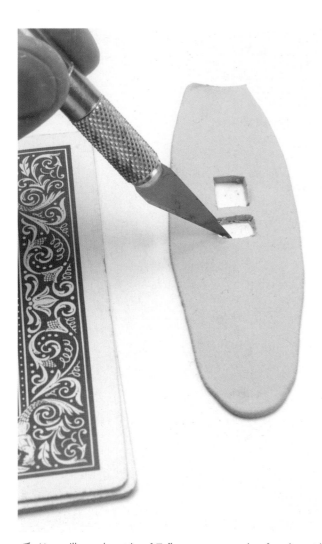

2 Roll out the base layer of clay about two cards thick. Dampen the surface with water and place the sheet with the cutouts over it. Press the layers to adhere.

1 You will need a strip of Teflon paper or a ring-forming strip that measures two sizes bigger than the finished ring size. Cut the strip a little longer than this measurement to overlap and join the ends with tape. It's helpful if you have a mandrel with ring sizes marked on it to get an accurate measurement. Put the taped strip on the mandrel.

This ring band is formed with two layers of clay: one layer with cutouts and one that will be the background. To make the layer with cutouts, roll out a sheet of clay three cards thick. Use the point of a knife to cut out rectangle shapes that will later be filled with cement. Dampen this piece or cover while you make the base piece.

3 Use a long blade to cut the strip of clay the width you desire and a little longer than the ring-forming strip on the mandrel. (It helps if the blade is lightly oiled to prevent sticking.)

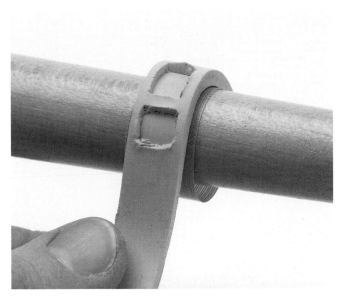

4 Wrap the clay strip loosely around the strip on the mandrel, overlapping the ends.

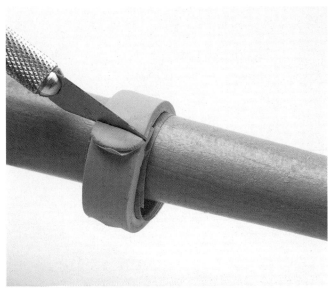

5 Use a knife or blade to cut through both layers at an angle. Remove the excess clay.

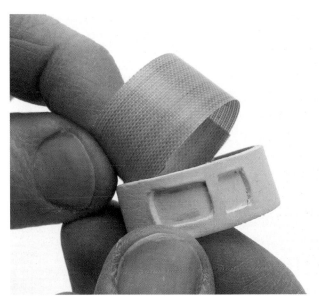

6 Use a clay shaper to blend the seam with a little water or slip. Let the ring dry on the mandrel for at least an hour. You can remove the ring from the mandrel and carefully remove the strip from the inside of the ring when the clay is firm enough to handle.

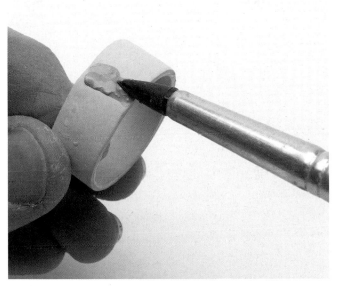

7 Continue to let the ring dry, making repairs to the seam as needed as it dries.

8 When the ring is bone dry, file the recessed shapes to define and neaten the edges with a needle file. Be careful when you handle the ring at this stage as it is very fragile.

9 Sand the edges of the ring in a circular motion on a flat piece of 400- or 600-grit sandpaper. Smooth the inside edges with sandpapers to round them slightly. Smooth the entire surface of the ring, brushing it with water as a final step before firing.

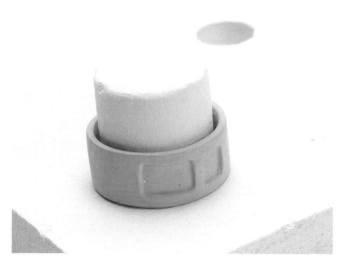

10 Place the ring on a kiln shelf with a ring form in the center. Fire at any temperature recommended for Art Clay Silver Slow Dry. Soak the fired piece in water and use a needle tool to remove the ring form, following the manufacturer's instructions. Rinse the ring and brass brush to burnish. Finish the ring as desired. (For extra strength, tumble the ring to work harden.)

11 Place a small amount of sculpting mixture (about 2 tablespoons) in a disposable cup. Mix with water, starting with a teaspoon and adding a few more drops at a time. Add a small amount of tinting paste with the water until the consistency is crumbly and stiff, yet holds together and can be molded like clay. Make sure the mixture is well mixed. Too little or too much water will weaken the final product.

Use a toothpick to fill the recessed areas with the prepared mixture. Press the cement with your fingers to level. Place the ring in a closed plastic bag for the first 24 hours to keep it from drying too quickly; this will strengthen the cement as it cures. After 24 hours, let it air dry to cure. This type of material will continue to cure for up to 28 days, although it will appear strong and can be handled after a few days. Hint: For extra strength, place a small piece of mesh made for use with cement (available from Winterstone) in the recessed area of the ring prior to adding the cement.

Creating Custom Closures

THIS CUFF BRACELET combines a woven wire pattern with textured silver clay. Fine silver wire is soft and pliable, making it ideal to crochet with, and the finished wire cuff is very soft and fabric-like. Metal clay is used to form edges that act as closures for the cuff, and the clay and crocheted wire are fired together. Use a type of metal clay that does not shrink very much, as shrinking will cause it to warp the wire. Don't despair if the edges warp a bit, though; this gives the cuff a soft organic look that complements the hand-crocheted wire.

TO MAKE ONE CUFF, YOU WILL NEED:

- PMC3
- Syringe clay or thick slip
- Basic metal clay supplies
- 28-gauge fine silver wire
- Size 5 metal crochet hook
- Wire cutters

- Mallet
- Bench block (Volcano Arts)
- Brass texture plates
- Faceted beads to embellish cuff
- Lobster-claw clasp
- Chain or jump rings to attach clasp

BEADED WIRE CUFF *by Sherri Haab*

1 (Note: The first three photos show the crocheted wire after several rows have been completed to give you a clearer idea of how the piece is formed.) To crochet the wire, work from the roll of wire starting a few inches from the end. Begin by making a chain stitch. (Follow steps 9 through 12 for the crocheted necklace on page 58 to make a chain stitch.) Crochet until the chain is about 5 1/2 inches long. Turn the chain around to begin a row of single crochet stitches along the chain. To begin a single crochet stitch, insert the hook into the second stitch from the hook. (The loop on the hook is coming out of the last stitch, so you don't want to insert the hook into this stitch. This counts as the first stitch, so hook into the next one.)

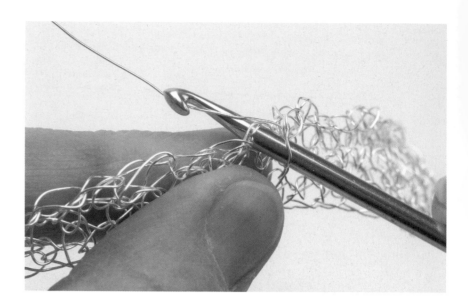

2 Hook the wire (wrap wire over the hook) and pull the wire through this chain stitch. Now you have two wire loops on the hook.

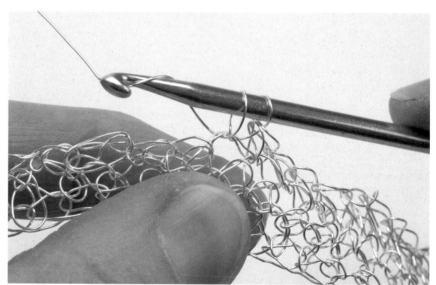

3 Hook the wire again. This time you will be pulling the wire through both loops on the hook. This completes one single crochet stitch, which will be the first stitch of your first row. Continue along the chain until you reach the last chain stitch. Before turning around to start a new row, make one extra chain stitch. This stitch is called the turning stitch. Flip the work over to start the next row.

To begin the next row, insert the hook into both loops of the first stitch. Make a single crochet stitch in each of the stitches along the row. (This photo shows the completed stitch with the wire pulled through both loops.)

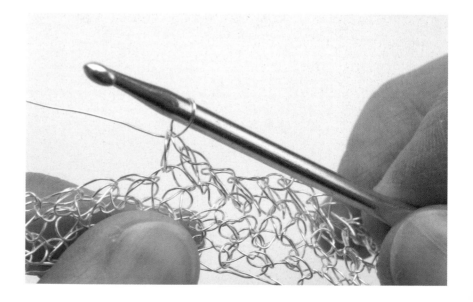

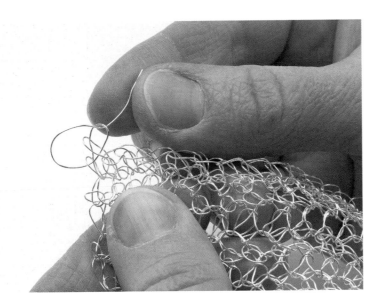

4 Keep crocheting rows until the cuff is as wide as you would like it, remembering to make a turning chain stitch at the end of each row. My finished cuff was about ten rows wide. Finish by clipping the end of the wire off a few inches from the end and pulling the wire through the last stitch.

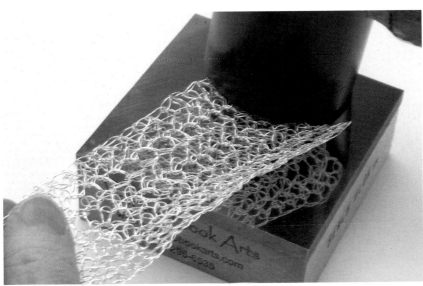

5 On a metal block or anvil use a mallet to flatten the ends of the cuff.

6 Roll out a sheet of metal clay about three cards thick and place it on the textured side of a brass texture plate. Cut one edge with a blade, to make a strip that is slightly wider than the edge of the crocheted wire cuff. Press the edge of the crocheted cuff into the clay with your fingers, leaving about 5/8 inch overlapping from the cut edge.

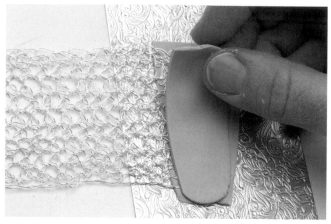

7 Roll out another sheet of clay and cut off the edges as you did in step 6. Align this cut edge with the previous edge of the clay, sandwiching the wire between. Add a little water between the layers to help the layers adhere if the clay has dried at all.

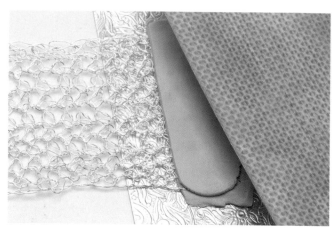

8 Place another texture plate, textured side down, on top of this sheet of clay.

9 Press down evenly on the brass texture plate to apply the texture to the clay.

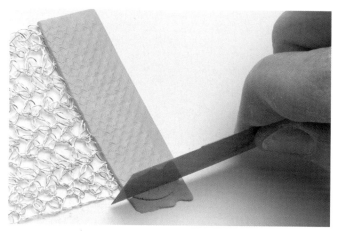

10 Trim the excess clay to align with the edges of the crocheted wire.

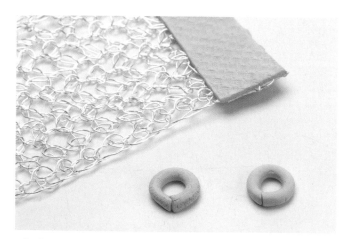

11 Make connections for the clasp by rolling small ropes of clay and forming the ropes into rings, one ring for each end of the cuff.

12 Attach the rings to each end of the cuff with syringe clay or thick slip. Use a clay shaper to blend the seam and secure the attachment.

13 Make decorative clay shapes to sew onto the wire cuff after firing: Roll out a sheet of clay about two to three cards thick and texture with a brass texture plate. Cut out shapes such as round disks. You can add smaller textured disk shapes to the center of larger shapes, using water to adhere.

14 Make holes around the edge of the finished shapes with a needle tool. These will be used to sew the finished shapes to the wire cuff.

Refine the edges of the cuff and cut shapes with a nail file or sandpapers. Use the tip of a knife to enlarge the holes if needed. Fire the wire cuff and decorative shapes in a kiln at any temperature recommended for PMC3.

15 Finish by brass brushing and polishing the silver clay ends with polishing papers. Patina the entire piece if desired. Remove some of the patina with a buffing pad or cloth. (Tumbling is not recommended as it makes the wire brittle and more prone to breaking.)

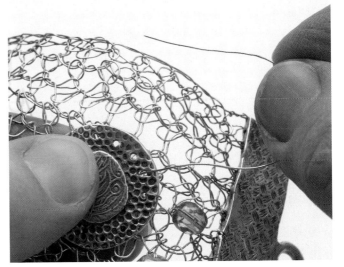

16 Use the same wire as you used for the crocheted cuff to sew the shapes onto the wire cuff. Sew beads onto the cuff to embellish. Twist the ends of the wires to secure to the cuff, hiding the ends inside the crocheted stitches.

Use pliers to attach a small length of chain and a lobster claw clasp to one side, measuring the clasp to make sure the cuff fits comfortably around your wrist.

Color, Images & Surface Design

A variety of art materials and techniques can be used to add color and excitement to your metal clay pieces. Glass and metal paints (acrylic enamels), image transfers, and resin are just a few. Some artists use nail polish, permanent markers, and colored pencils, pushing the limit of what you can use to add color to metal. Adhering gold sheet or firing high-karat liquid gold with silver is yet another way to add a variety to the surface of the metal and create geometric or painterly effects.

Framing a Transparency Film Image

GOLD LEAF shining through a layer of transparency film and resin gives this piece depth and dimension. Artist Cassy Muronaka, who designed this piece, suggests using an image with strong lines, but not a lot of detail (faces are perfect). Gold leaf darkens the image, so it's best to lighten the image before printing the transparency.

TO MAKE ONE PIN, YOU WILL NEED:

- PMC Standard
- PMC slip
- PMC syringe clay
- Basic metal clay supplies
- PolyBlade clay-cutting blade (AMACO)
- Dried bits of clay
- HattieS sterling silver pin back (PMC Supply; optional)
- Color image
- Transparency film (8 1/2 by 11 inches)
- Sobo glue
- Gold leaf
- Epoxy resin (Envirotex Lite)
- Mixing cups and toothpick for resin

The template on the left is for the background; the one on the right is for the "frame."

BOTTICELLI PENDANT AND RUSSIAN ICON PIN *by Cassy Muronaka*

The steps that follow show how to make the Russian icon pin. You can use the frame pattern provided or design your own to fit the image you choose.

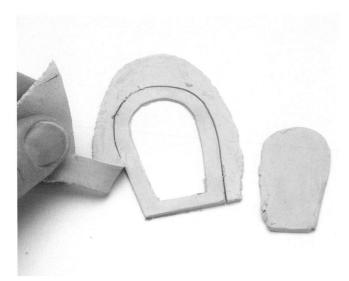

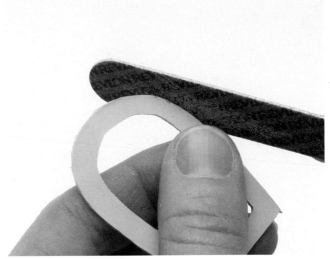

1 Copy and cut out the paper patterns for the pin. PMC Standard shrinks 25 to 30 percent, so the pattern will be much bigger than the final piece. To make the frame piece, roll out a sheet of clay four cards thick on a nonstick surface and cut out the shape using the frame pattern. Remove the excess clay and set aside to dry.

2 When the frame is dry, refine the edges with a nail file or sandpapers. Remember that the frame is fragile at this stage.

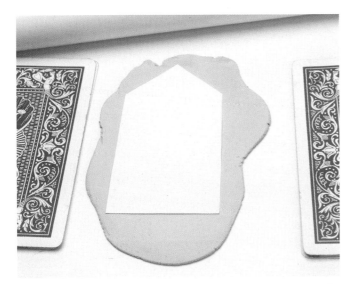

3 To create the foundation, roll out a sheet of clay three cards thick and cut out the shape using the pattern.

4 Attach the frame to the foundation using a layer of slip to attach. Press the frame with your fingers to adhere.

5 To add a texture around the frame, chop up bits of dried clay with a blade until fine.

6 Brush slip thickly around the frame; this will hold the chopped clay in place.

7 Working with one section at a time, add chopped clay to the slip and press to adhere. Add more slip as needed and continue adding chopped clay until the entire area around the frame is covered.

8 Let the piece dry thoroughly, then sand and refine the edges as needed. Fire the piece face down on a kiln shelf at 1650°F for 2 hours. To add a pin back after firing, attach the finding with syringe clay before burnishing the piece. Fire again for 30 minutes at a temperature no higher than 1470°F. Alternatively, you could add a loop to hang the piece, as shown in this photo.

After firing, finish the silver with a brass brush. Add a patina and buff and burnish the piece to leave the patina in the recessed areas of the texture.

9 Note: Your image will be printed on the rough or "un-shiny" side of the transparency paper. If your image has text, print the image backwards as the orientation of the transparency will be shiny side up when finished. Scan the image you want to frame and make a few test copies to determine how to size the image. Use a photo program to make adjustments to the image if needed. Insert a sheet of transparency film in your printer and print out the image. You may want to print a few extra images of varying size and lightness to give you options, or to have extras in case you make a mistake in cutting or sizing. Print the image and hold it over your frame to check size and placement.

10 Place the transparency over the frame and use a permanent marker to trace around the inside of the frame.

11 Flip the transparency over and brush a thin layer of glue on the printed side. Let this dry until the glue is clear but still tacky (about 20 to 30 minutes).

12 Place the image glued side down on a sheet of gold leaf. Press to adhere. Pull or brush away the excess leaf.

13 Cut around the marked line to fit the frame. Brush a thin layer of glue inside the frame and press the image into the frame. Let the glue dry completely.

14 Follow manufacturer's directions to mix the epoxy resin. Mix well to ensure proper curing; it's always best to transfer the mixture into a second cup and mix again right before application. Use a toothpick to add the resin to the frame, coaxing the resin around the inside of the frame until the entire image is covered. Use a heat gun to remove any bubbles on the surface. Let the resin cure in a warm spot undisturbed at least overnight or for several days.

Coloring Silver with Resin

THIS PROJECT combines the beauty of fine silver with colorful resin and polymer clay. Using colored resin to fill cells on metal is often referred to as "cold enameling," because the result looks similar to traditional glass enamel. Glitter and other inclusions can be added to the resin to lend texture and variety to the piece.

TO MAKE ONE BRACELET, YOU WILL NEED:

- PMC+
- Basic metal clay supplies
- 5/16-inch teardrop-shaped cutter (Kemper tools)
- 3/4-inch teardrop-shaped cutter (Kemper tools)
- Forget-me-not-shaped cutter (Kemper tools)
- Leather-stamping tool
- Colored epoxy resin in pink, orange, white, and green (Colores)
- Clear epoxy resin (Colores)
- Mixing cups for resin

- Toothpicks or old paintbrush
- Beedz™ (Art Accentz™)
- Glitter
- Freshwater pearls (6 mm)
- Silver head pins with ball ends
- Purchased silver charm bracelet with loop and toggle closure
- Silver jump rings
- Round-nose pliers
- Wire cutters
- Various colors of polymer clay (optional)

SPRING FLOWERS CHARM BRACELET *by Sherri Haab*

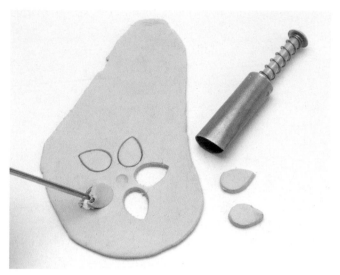

1 Begin by making the large flowers that will be colored with resin. Roll out a sheet of clay, three playing cards thick, on a nonstick surface. Use the pointed end of a paintbrush or a toothpick to make a mark to designate the center of the flower in the sheet of clay. Cut out petal shapes with the small teardrop cutter to make five petals around the mark. Take care to space them evenly.

2 Roll out another sheet of clay, three cards thick, for the base or backing piece. Brush water between the two sheets of clay and place the sheet with the petal cutouts on top of the base sheet of clay. Press the layers to adhere.

3 Use a knife to cut out the outside of the flower shape, cutting through both layers. Leave enough clay around each petal to create a bezel for holding the resin. Allow for extra space at the point of one of the petals to form a hole for hanging. Use olive oil to prevent the clay from sticking to the knife. Remove the excess clay.

4 Use a needle tool to form a hole in the petal with the most room at the point. Don't worry about the hole being the perfect size; you can refine this later.

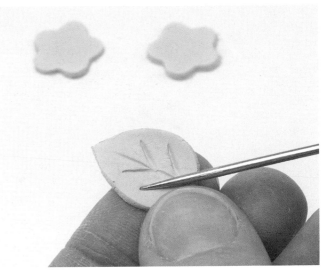

5 Use slip to attach a small ball of clay to the center of each flower. Use a leather-stamping tool to press a design into the center, which will also help attach the ball firmly to the center of the flower. Make two more flowers in the same way, then set the flowers on a flat surface to dry.

6 Roll out a sheet of clay, three cards thick, and cut out leaf shapes using the larger teardrop-shaped cutter. Make veins with a needle tool.

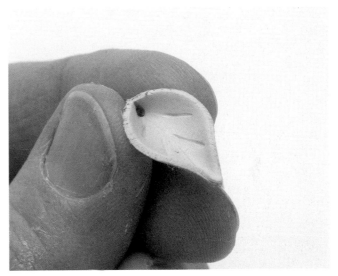

7 Gently fold up the edges of each metal clay leaf to make a cup shape.

8 Use a needle tool to make a hole at the top of each leaf for hanging. Let the leaves dry.

9 Cut flower shapes out of a sheet of clay, three cards thick, with the forget-me-not-shaped cutter. Use a needle tool to form lines that radiate out from the center and make a hole in the center of flower. Shape the flowers with a pointed tool and let dry.

Sand the edges of all the clay pieces with a nail file, followed by sandpapers, until smooth. Use a small drill bit or the point of a craft knife to "drill" and refine the holes in the pieces. Smooth with water using your finger or a paintbrush.

Fire the pieces on a kiln shelf at any of the temperatures recommended for PMC+. Burnish the flowers and leaves with a brass brush followed by sandpapers. Finish by polishing in a tumbler until shiny.

10 To color the petals of the large flowers, mix the colored resin according to the manufacturer's instructions. (Colores brand resin uses two parts resin to one part hardener.) Hot pink and orange were each tinted with white to create the flower colors for this project. Use a toothpick to place a single drop of colored resin into each petal to coat the bottom of the petal. Let the resin set under a warm light for several hours.

11 Mix a batch of clear resin and drop into each petal as you did with the colored resin. The colored resin layer does not need to be fully cured as you add the clear resin; both layers will continue to cure together.

12 Sprinkle glitter or other small inclusions (such as Beedz) into the resin while it is still liquid. Attach jump rings to the leaves before adding resin. Mix a drop of green resin with clear resin to create a very pale green. Add the ratio of hardener needed to the green resin and mix well. Drop the resin into the leaves until the resin fills the leaves. Let the resin set in a warm place for several days until cured.

Add jump rings to the flowers after the resin has cured and attach them to the charm bracelet. Attach the leaves to the chain between the flowers.

13 To add small pearls to the centers of the small silver flowers, thread a pearl onto a head pin. Add a silver flower and make a loop on the back with round-nose pliers to attach to the charm bracelet. Twist the wire to secure and clip off the excess.

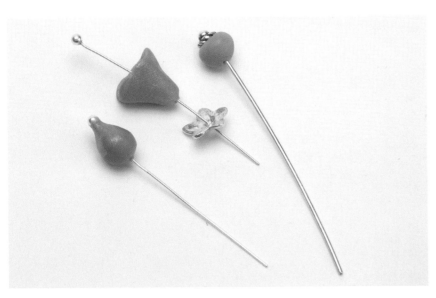

14 If you want to add extra elements to the bracelet as shown on the front cover of this book, you can thread small balls of polymer clay (to resemble flowers and buds) onto head pins and bake at 275°F for 30 minutes. Use round-nose pliers to create loops in the head pins to attach to the bracelet.

You can also form metal clay beads over cork balls and decorate them with tiny balls of clay attached with slip. Attach the beads to the bracelet with fancy head pins to further embellish.

Painting on Silver

ARTIST CASSY MURONAKA created this fun look by coloring recessed areas in fired metal clay with colorful transparent paints that are formulated to be used on nonporous surfaces. Cassy's use of recessed areas in her design helps to protect the paint from wear. The paint has little chance of being scraped or scratched off. The great thing about this type of paint is that colors stay true and vibrant over time.

TO MAKE ONE NECKLACE AND PAIR OF EARRINGS, YOU WILL NEED:

- PMC+
- Paste or slip
- Basic metal clay supplies
- 3/4-inch round circle cutter (Kemper tools)
- 3/16-inch round circle cutter (Kemper tools)
- Pin vise with drill bits
- Paint Jewels™ Glossy Colors™ (Delta)
- Several round toothpicks
- Nine 6mm silver jump rings
- Silver-plated or sterling silver necklace chain for necklace (length of choice)
- Silver ear wires for earrings
- Small length of chain for earrings
- Pliers

DOT NECKLACE AND EARRINGS *by Cassy Muronaka*

To make a necklace, add jump rings to seven painted silver circles and attach to a purchased chain with pliers. For earrings, use two jump rings to attach two circles to a small length of chain for each (about 1 1/2 inches long). Attach the chains to ear wires to finish.

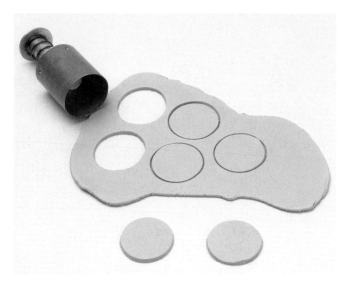

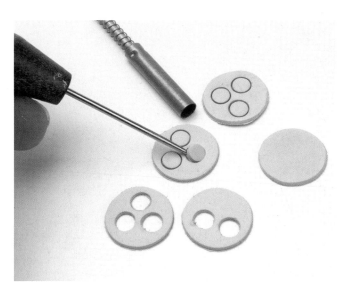

1 Roll out a sheet of PMC, three playing cards thick, on a Teflon sheet or other nonstick surface. Use the ³/₄-inch circle cutter to cut out circles of clay. You will need seven circles for a necklace and two circles for earrings. Keep the cut circles moist and covered with plastic wrap if necessary to prevent drying as you prepare for the next step.

2 Cut a few small "polka dots" within each of the clay circle cutouts using the ³/₁₆-inch circle cutter. These will be the largest dots for the design. Leave room for smaller dots to be added in the next step. Let the circles dry.

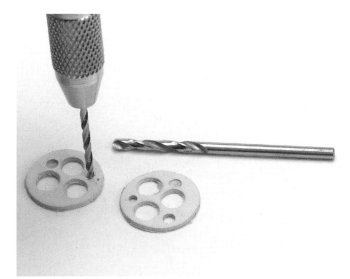

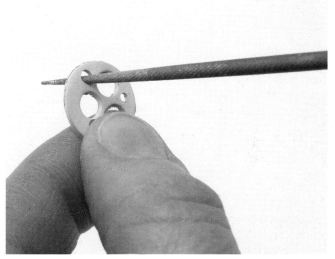

3 When your clay circles are leather-hard, use a pin vise with a drill bit to make smaller dots between the large dots. Vary the sizes of the dots and place them randomly. One of these holes should be near the border, where your jump ring will pass through for hanging. Remember to allow for shrinkage so that the jump ring will pass through the hole after firing. Take your time drilling, being careful not to force the drill bit through the clay or put pressure on the clay, which might cause it to break.

4 Use a small round needle file or rolled up sandpaper to gently refine and smooth the inside edges of the cut and drilled dots. The pieces are very fragile at this stage. Be careful not to apply too much pressure as you sand.

5 Roll out a sheet of PMC, two playing cards thick. Cut out circles with the larger circle cutter as you did in step 1. These will act as the backing circles for the dried dotted circles. Dampen the freshly cut circles with a layer of slip. Press the dried dot circles onto each one. Press to make sure the layers adhere well. Let the pieces dry until bone dry.

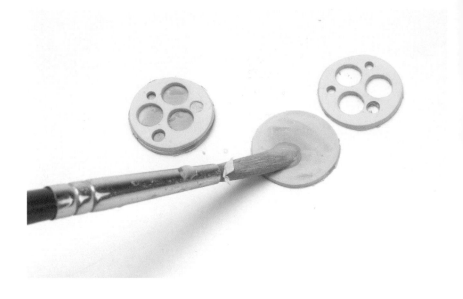

6 After the circles have dried, use a nail file and fine sandpapers to smooth and even up the outer edges of the finished circles. Drill through the hole designated for the jump ring on each shape, making sure to drill all the way through the back layer. Refine the hole with a round file or rolled sandpaper if needed.

   Fire the circles on a kiln shelf according to any of the temperatures recommended for PMC+. After firing, brass brush and sand using progressively finer papers for a mirror finish. For extra shine, tumble the circles for about 40 minutes. Finish by polishing the silver with a buffing cloth.

7 Apply a variety of paint colors to each of the recessed dots. Use a toothpick to "drop" small amounts of paint into each little round dot. Use a different toothpick for each color, or wipe off the toothpick between colors with a tissue. Allow the paint to dry according to the manufacturer's instructions. If you accidentally get paint outside of the dots, you can scratch it off with your fingernail after the paint has dried.

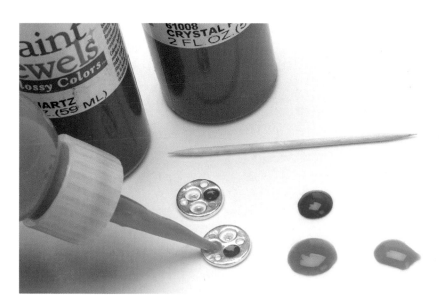

Liquid Medium Image Transfer

THIS INNOVATIVE TECHNIQUE produces an ethereal, transparent image as the silver shines through what was the unprinted, or "white," area of the image, while the color from the image remains on the silver. You may want to practice on a few old bottle caps before working with fine silver, as the images often look different on paper than they do when applied to metal. Sometimes the border or edges of the image are a little irregular. I find these "imperfections" add beauty and character to the piece.

TO MAKE ONE BRACELET, YOU WILL NEED:

- PMC+ or PMC3
- Basic metal clay supplies
- Leather-stamping tool
- Image printed with a toner-based copier or printer
- Image Transfer Solution™ (Sherri Haab Designs or PMC Supply)
- Renaissance Wax (PMC Supply)
- Chain for the bracelet
- Box clasp
- Pliers

IMAGE TRANSFER BRACELET *by Sherri Haab*

1 Roll out a sheet of clay, four cards thick. Cut a rectangle plaque for the bracelet. This one is about 1 1/4 inches tall by 1 1/2 inches wide. Use a needle tool to pierce four holes in each side to attach the chain later. Texture the edge of the piece with a leather-stamping tool if desired. Drape the piece over a mug to dry; this will give the finished piece a nice curved shape.

2 After the piece has dried, use a nail file to lightly sand the edges and round the corners. Use the point of a craft knife to neaten up the holes. Fire the piece on a fiber blanket to maintain the curve. Fire at any of the temperatures recommended for PMC+ or PMC3.

Use a brass brush to burnish the piece after firing. Use 600-grit wet/dry sandpaper or fine steel wool to refine the surface. The surface should have a bit of "tooth" to it, so don't sand the metal to a mirror finish.

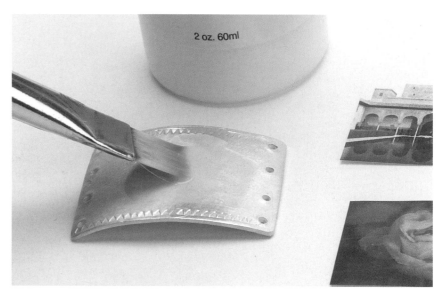

3 Make sure the metal is clean and free of oil or dirt. To apply an image, brush an even layer (not too thin) of image transfer solution on the surface of the metal with a flat brush.

Press the image face down onto the solution. (Note: Saturated colors work best. If text is used, print a mirror image as the transfer will reverse the image.) Carefully press from the center out to make sure the image is in full contact with the surface of the metal. Press out any air bubbles. Remove any solution that oozes out from the edges with a toothpick. Let the piece dry thoroughly.

4 Place the piece in a preheated oven and bake at 325°F for 40 minutes. Remove the piece from the oven and let cool, then soak in warm water for about 10 minutes. Gently rub the back of the paper off with your fingers, starting in the center and working outwards. Dip the piece in water as you work to keep the paper soaked. Be careful not to scrape the edges of the image as you continue to remove all traces of paper. There may be a bit of paper fibers remaining, appearing as a film on the surface as it dries. Carefully sand the surface with 600-grit wet/dry sandpaper to remove, using water to lubricate and gliding the paper across the surface in one direction; don't scrub. Work with a light hand to avoid scratching the image.

5 To protect and seal the image, use a soft cloth to buff the surface with a layer of wax. The wax will bring up the luster and help to hide any traces of fibers that remain. Let it dry and repeat with a second coat. Attach jump rings, a chain, and a clasp with pliers to complete the bracelet.

Lazertran Image Transfer

IN THIS PROJECT by Wendy Wallin Malinow, a hollow silver bezel is filled with polymer clay, and images are transferred to the polymer clay on both sides to create a reversible pendant: Two necklaces for the price of one! You can use the illustration provided here or one of your own—even a photo.

TO MAKE ONE PENDANT, YOU WILL NEED:

- PMC3
- Basic metal clay supplies
- Cork clay
- Paper patterns (copied and cut out)
- Sobo glue
- 2 ounces white or pearl polymer clay (Premo/Polyform Products)
- One sheet of Lazertran Silk
- Small bits of colored polymer clay to embellish piece
- Glass rhinestones
- Gloss glaze (Sculpey/Polyform Products; optional)
- Chain or leather cord

REVERSIBLE FLOWER PENDANT *by Wendy Wallin Malinow*

Patterns for reversible flower pendant.

1 To make a template for the bezel, copy one of the flower patterns in black and white and cut around the shape. (Reduce the size if you want a smaller pendant.) Roll out a thick sheet of cork clay (about ¹/₄ inch thick) and lay the pattern on top of the cork. Cut around the shape with the point of a craft knife. Cut with an up-and-down sawing motion to get a clean edge. Use a clay shaper or the tip of a pencil to refine the small recessed areas between the petals.

2 Let the piece dry thoroughly. You can sand any rough areas after the cork is dry. Lightly coat the edges of the cork with glue and let dry until tacky.

3 Roll out a sheet of metal clay, three cards thick, to make the bezel. Cut strips ¼ inch wide and carefully wrap the strips around the glued edges of the form. When you need to join one strip to the next, blend the seams well with a clay shaper or your fingers. A playing card works well to help work the strips of clay into tight areas. Watch as the piece dries to add extra clay at each seam if a line appears.

4 Decorate the edges with small balls of clay attached with slip and use a needle tool to make a dot in the middle of each. Add texture around the raised dots with the needle tool if desired.

Wrap a small strip of clay, ¼ inch wide, around a straw to create a bezel for the cord to go through. Let it dry, then slide it off the straw and sand the edges on a flat sheet of sandpaper. (To hang the pendant with a chain from each side, make two bezels.)

Sand any rough edges of the flower-shaped bezel and check for cracks. Let all the clay pieces dry, then fire them at 1472°F for 30 minutes at a ramp speed of 1500°F per hour. After the pieces cool, brass brush and tumble for extra strength.

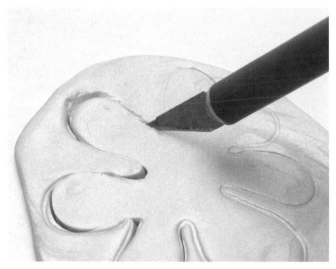

5 To use the provided illustration, scan and reduce a test copy to size the image to fit the flower bezel. When you have the correct size, take the illustrations to a copy shop and have the illustrations copied in color on a sheet of Lazertran Silk. (The copies need to be made with a toner-based copier, not an ink-jet printer.) Make sure the copy is printed on the side that has a slight sheen.

Condition the polymer clay and roll it out to the thickness of the bezel. Lightly press the bezel into the clay to impress the bezel outline for cutting. Use a craft knife to cut out the shape.

6 Press the clay into the open bezel using your fingers to smooth the clay around all of the edges. As you are pressing the clay into the bezel, be careful not to bend the silver; work slowly and gently to fit the clay into place. Trim away any excess clay and smooth again until the clay is level on both sides of the bezel. Set the piece aside as you prepare the transfer.

7 Cut out the transfers and burnish the first one on the corresponding side of the clay. First smooth with your finger to adhere, then use the back of a spoon to burnish the entire surface for full contact. Repeat on the other side with the remaining image. Let the piece set for 30 minutes.

Put the piece in a shallow pan of water, holding the edges of the bezel with your fingers. Within a minute or two the backing of the Lazertran paper will float off both sides. Don't peel the paper off; it will release from the clay by itself. Remove the piece from the water and gently pat (don't rub) the surface with a paper towel to remove water droplets.

8 Let the piece dry undisturbed for about 1 hour. Balance the edges of the silver bezel on pieces of cardboard to protect the image on the back as the piece dries.

9 Place the piece on a sheet of waxed paper to protect the black-and-white image on the back. Press small pieces of clay and glass rhinestones into the colored side to decorate. Using a round cutter that corresponds to the diameter of the round bezel you created in step 4, cut a hole in the polymer clay to add the bezel for hanging. (If you made two bezels in step 4, make two holes in the flower.) Insert the bezel and smooth the edges of the clay to surround it. Be careful not to rub so hard that the image is disturbed; it's still fragile until it is heat set.

10 Preheat the oven to 275°F and prop the piece up on edge in a baking dish, using a piece of cardboard to prevent it from slipping. Anchor the cardboard with a bit of unbaked polymer clay to keep it firmly in place. This will keep the transfer on the back suspended as it bakes, as it will stick to the glass if it touches. Bake the pieces for 30 minutes. Let it cool in the oven.

Seal the image with gloss glaze to further protect the images or to give a glossy sheen to the surface. Add a cord or chain to complete the pendant.

Silver & Gold

PEACOCK RING *by Hattie Sanderson*
PMC3 and PMC Gold combine to provide a rich setting for an exquisite peacock topaz. (Photo by the artist.)

HOLLOW FORM BOX BRACELET *by Celie Fago*
Celie used keum-boo to accent this bracelet of PMC, 18-karat gold, and sterling silver. (Photo by Robert Diamante.)

GOLD METAL CLAY is a high-karat gold with a rich, warm, yellow color. It can be sculpted, fired, and finished in the same fashion as silver metal clay. Using pure gold in a project can be expensive, especially when used by itself. Fortunately, there are several options for combining high-karat gold with silver and new formulations of gold that can be fired along with silver. Using various gold products gives you the opportunity to feature pure gold in your work without having to spend a fortune.

Aura 22 (from PMC) is a thin gold "slip" with the consistency of cream. It can be painted on fired silver metal clay or sterling silver to create a 22-karat-gold finish. AGS™ Accent Gold for Silver™ is a fine gold (24-karat) powder that you mix with a medium to create a gold paint that can also be applied to fired silver. After applying either product, refire the silver and burnish to the desired finish.

You can also plate silver with high-karat gold by means of a battery-operated pen, which is used to apply a 24-karat-gold plating solution. This method does not require refiring. (See "Firing Silver with Dichroic Glass" on page 84 for use of this pen.)

Keum-boo is another method of incorporating high-karat gold and silver. This technique involves heating a fired metal clay piece to bond pure gold sheet to the surface. By cutting the sheet with scissors or paper punches, you can control the edges of the gold, producing crisp detailed lines and shapes. Many jewelry artists use touches of keum-boo to add geometric details to silver pieces.

QUATRE FLEUR
DE LIS NECKLACE #8
by Shahasp Valentine
A sapphire set in
24-karat PMC Gold
forms the focal point
of this necklace made
of silver PMC, pearls,
and a 24-karat-gold
chain. (Photo by
the artist.)

SEGMENTED
BUTTERFLY
by Kelly Russell
Gold sheet applied
to the top right
segment of this metal
clay bead using the
technique of keum-
boo enhances the
delicate butterfly
motif. (Photo by
Robert Diamante.)

Painting Gold on Silver

APPLYING AURA 22 to fired silver clay creates dainty petal shapes that are silver on the outside and gold on the inside. For a rich gold color, apply two or three even coats of Aura 22. (I used two coats on this necklace.) Freshwater pearls complement the organic look of these handmade petals. You can even see your fingerprints in each petal, which adds a subtle surface texture.

TO MAKE ONE NECKLACE, YOU WILL NEED:

- PMC+
- Aura 22
- Basic metal clay supplies
- Paintbrush for gold
- Head pins
- Pearls
- Round-nose pliers
- Wire clippers
- Purchased necklace chain

GOLD PETAL NECKLACE *by Sherri Haab*

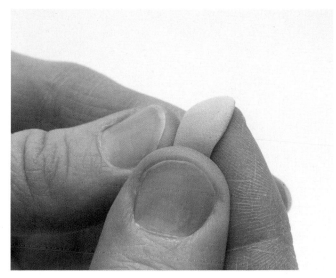

1 Pinch off a small ball of clay and press it into a flat pad on your fingertip. Press the edges with your thumb to form a cupped shape on your finger.

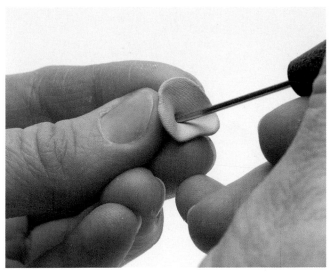

2 Use a clay shaper to make an indentation in the center of the clay and form a hole in the center with a needle tool. Make as many petal shapes as you would like on your necklace and let dry. You can vary the size of the petals if desired. Fire the pieces at any of the temperatures recommended for PMC+.

3 Do not burnish or brush the fired pieces before applying the gold solution. Stir the Aura 22 solution with a needle tool until mixed. It should be the consistency of cream. Using a clean brush dedicated for the gold, apply an even layer to the inside surface of each petal shape. Let the pieces dry, then apply a second coat in the same manner. Add a drop of thinner, which comes with the product, as needed to keep the consistency of the solution cream-like, but not too thin.

4 Fire the painted petal shapes in a kiln at 850°F for 30 minutes. Burnish the petals with a brass brush to bring up the shine of the gold and silver.

5 Place a pearl on a head pin and thread the pin through the center of a petal.

6 Bend the end of the head pin with pliers to form a 90-degree angle.

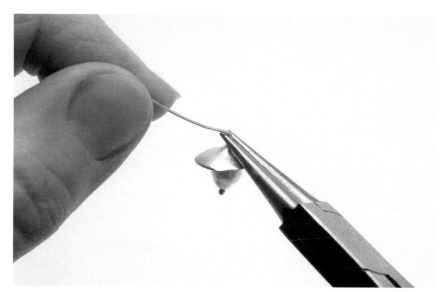

7 Make a loop in the head pin with round-nose pliers. Attach this loop to a purchased chain and wrap the end of the head pin around the base of the loop to finish. Clip off the excess wire. Continue adding petals with pearls to the chain to create a design. Hint: Arrange the larger petal shapes in the center of the necklace, with the petals becoming smaller as they progress up each side.

Keum-boo Technique

KEUM-BOO is the ancient Asian technique of bonding 24-karat-gold foil to the surface of metal, usually fine silver. Freshly fired metal clay is perfectly suited for keum-boo, because it needs little preparation. Artist Celie Fago has developed keum-boo techniques for PMC, using the Ultra-Lite Beehive Kiln. In this project, the kiln is used to fire the silver clay, then, with the use of a brass element (keum-boo cover), it serves as a "hot plate" to bond the gold foil to the surface of the silver. The instructions for this project are based on techniques developed by Celie Fago and described in her book, *Keum-boo on Silver*.

TO MAKE ONE PAIR OF EARRINGS, YOU WILL NEED:

- PMC+ or PMC3
- Basic metal clay tools
- Lace or textured rubber stamp
- Clay pattern cutter (Klay Kutters)
- Gold foil (Allcraft or Rio Grande; do not use gold leaf or enameling foil)
- Sharp scissors
- A sheet of plain copy paper
- Two steel ball-end or agate burnishers
- Fine tweezers or cross-lock tweezers
- Leather gloves
- Ear wires
- Head pins and beads (optional)

KEUM-BOO EARRINGS *by Sherri Haab*
Earrings with a sparkle of silver and gold are the perfect project to try your hand at keum-boo.

1 Roll out a sheet of clay three cards thick and add a texture to the clay with lace or an oiled rubber stamp. Cut out round shapes with a clay pattern cutter and use a needle tool to pierce the shapes at the top for hanging. If you want to add bead dangles to the earrings, pierce a hole at the bottom of each shape.

2 Place the shapes over a slightly curved surface such as a light-bulb to dry. After the pieces are dry, refine the edges with a nail file or sandpapers. Enlarge the holes with the tip of a knife to clean them up.

Fire the pieces in the Ultra-Lite Beehive Kiln. Be sure to read all of the firing and safety instructions before using the kiln. The kiln should be preheated for 35 minutes (covered with the firing insert in place). Place the dried metal clay pieces on the heated insert and fire (uncovered) for either of these schedules: 30 minutes for PMC+ or 20 minutes for PMC3. Let the pieces cool after firing; they will be extremely hot. The pieces should remain in a freshly fired, unburnished state.

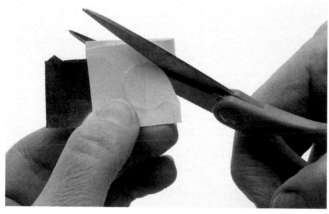

3 To make a pattern for the gold foil pieces to be cut, press one of the fired silver pieces against a small piece of folded paper. Make a rubbing over the texture of the silver piece with the paper to see the shape of the form. Remove the silver piece and slip the gold foil inside the folded paper. Use sharp, pointed scissors to cut out the desired shape. In this case a half-moon shape was cut to fit the dimensions of the rubbing. Cutting the foil between paper sheets also helps to keep the foil from tearing or from sticking in the scissors. Hint: Try to conserve as much foil as possible when cutting the shape.

Keum-boo Safety Tips

Because you will be working over a heated area, safety is of the utmost importance. Follow these safety guidelines before working over the hot element:

- If you have long hair, tie it back.
- Wear well-fitting leather gloves. (Leather garden gloves work well for this purpose.)
- Wear an apron and leather shoes (not sandals).
- Make sure the area is free of flammable objects and place a tile under and next to the kiln.
- If using a work light, place the light at an angle, not directly above the kiln.
- Attend to the kiln at all times. Never leave it, even for a moment.

4 Place the kiln on a table at a height that will let you work without bending over. If needed, add a heavy-duty (16-gauge) extension cord that is not more than 6 feet long. Heat the kiln with the keum-boo cover in place. After about 20 minutes, the temperature will reach between 745°F and 850°F, which is the ideal temperature for keum-boo.

Place one earring shape on the keum-boo cover; use tweezers to avoid getting too close to the heat. (This piece has a slight curve and is placed on the flat area. If your piece is more domed, place it in the recessed area where the heat will surround it better.) Wearing gloves, use tweezers to place the gold. Make an initial tack in the middle of the gold shape with a burnisher.

5 Burnish the gold in a circular motion with medium pressure. (A ball-end burnisher works well to tack small crevices on a textured surface.) Work from the center outward. Burnish the surface of the gold firmly onto the silver, paying special attention to the edges of the gold, and being careful not to trap air as you move from the middle out to the edges. This photo shows an agate burnisher being used with a steel burnisher; you can use two steel burnishers instead. Hint: If you're using a steel burnisher, and it begins to feel "sticky," stop and swap burnishers, or pause for a few moments to let the burnisher cool.

6 Continue burnishing to bond the gold to the surface, including any crevices. Add small pieces of gold to repair tears or bald spots (overlapping is fine). Don't worry about burnishing marks; they will disappear when you finish the piece.

When you're finished adding gold, remove your piece promptly, or the gold will continue to diffuse into the surface. (Note: Diffusion begins after about 10 minutes; the gold begins to pale as it is "absorbed" into the silver. If the gold is diffused more than you like, you can add a patina at the end, which will help emphasize the contrast.)

Allow the piece to cool, but don't submerge it in water. Hold the cooled piece up to a light and examine the surface, especially the borders of the attached gold. Run your fingernail along the edges of the gold and try to lift it. If you feel an edge, the gold is not attached well. Simply reheat the piece and reburnish.

7 Repeat the process for the other earring piece. When you are finished applying the foil, remove the burnishing marks in any of the following ways. Brass brush the pieces with or without mild soapy water; if you will go on to patina the piece, this is the right preparation. If you're not going to add a patina, you can enhance the look of the gold by rubbing the piece with a little pumice powder on a dampened finger. This increases the contrast between the gold and silver, enhancing the color of the gold. You may also tumble-polish the pieces. However, by increasing the shine, tumbling will lessen the contrast between the gold and the silver, and the gold will be harder to discern.

Attach ear wires to the finished pieces and add bead dangles with head pins, if desired.

Contributing Artists

THE FOLLOWING ARTISTS have generously allowed me to show their work in this book or contributed projects. Most of them have websites at which you can contact them or view more of their jewelry.

KAREN L. COHEN Karen is a jewelry designer who specializes in cloisonné enameling on fine silver. Her work frequently incorporates fine silver and gold wires, transparent leaded vitreous enamels, and Precious Metal Clay and features surface textures and abstract designs. Karen also creates other enameled items such as stamp boxes, flatware, dishes, and photo holders. She is the author of the book *The Art of Fine Enameling* (Sterling, 2002). *www.kcenamels.com*

ROBERT DANCIK Robert holds degrees in sculpture and fine art and has been an artist and teacher for more than thirty years. His jewelry and sculpture have been exhibited in museums and galleries across the United States and in Japan. He teaches workshops at art centers in the U.S. and abroad, and his work is featured in numerous books and magazines. Robert is the originator of Faux Bone™, a wonderful new material for book artists, jewelers, and other artists. He lives in Oxford, Connecticut, where he is an avid cook and collector of toys, maps, and compasses. *www.robertdancik.com*

CELIE FAGO Celie's work combines PMC with polymer clay and metals. She is highly regarded as an innovator in the combination of these materials and as a generous teacher. Celie is one of eight senior instructors with the Rio Rewards Certification Program. In addition to writing numerous articles on PMC and polymer clay, she collaborated with Tim McCreight on the video, *Push Play for PMC: Intermediate Techniques* (PMC Guild, 2001). Her latest book is *Keum-boo on Silver* (self-published, 2004). *www.celiefago.com*

RIGHT: CONCRETE PENDANT *by Robert Dancik*
A bezel made from metal clay is an elegant setting for tinted concrete. (Photo by Douglas Foulke.)

FAR RIGHT: TRIANGLE BOX PENDANT *by Celie Fago*
Celie used the technique of keum-boo to add 24-karat gold to PMC to this striking pendant.

PATTI LEOTA GENACK Patti started her artistic career as a printmaker, earning an MFA in printmaking from the University of Oregon. She eventually moved on to life-size figurative charcoals and then mixed media sculpture. Sculpture was Patti's segue into making glass beads and working in PMC. Once she started working in those two mediums, she was hooked, and all her artistic energies are now devoted to the jewelry arts. *www.whimwhambeads.com*

LORA HART Lora Hart began working with metal clay six years ago when an actor's strike put her twenty-year career as a makeup artist in the entertainment industry on hold. Self-taught at first, Lora began formal training in traditional jewelrymaking at various schools in Los Angeles and went on to complete four metal clay certification programs. She has been committed to furthering her knowledge and skill in this alchemous art form ever since. Lora is also a contributing writer for *Step by Step Beads* and *Studio PMC* magazines. *www.lorahart.com*

SUSAN GIFFORD KNOPP Susan developed her love of bright colors during her high school years on the island of Oahu, Hawaii. She dabbled in etching, painting, metalsmithing, and furniture making, but eventually began to work in cloisonné enamel while attending California State University at Sacramento. Susan works in two different styles, whimsical realism and abstraction, and she often includes images of women in her pieces. *www.susanknoppenamels.com*

WENDY WALLIN MALINOW Wendy spent her early career as an art director and graphic designer. In 1989, she began to pursue freelance illustration full time. She started working with beads in the late '80s and has continued designing jewelry ever since. She

FELTED PURSE
by Michelle Ross
Think beyond jewelry when designing metal clay and mixed media pieces. Here, metal clay embellishes a felted purse knit with various yarns.

has contributed to many art publications and various craft books, and her work appears in *400 Polymer Clay Designs* (Lark, 2004) and *500 Necklaces* (Lark, 2006). Wendy has won awards in advertising, book illustration, and jewelry design and has exhibited at numerous galleries and shows. She continues to explore combining metal with alternative materials. You can contact her at eyefun@comcast.net.

CASSY MURONAKA Cassy Muronaka is a former *Los Angeles Times* staff photographer and *United Press International* reporter who has been working with polymer clay for fifteen years. Her work was recently featured in *400 Polymer Clay Designs* (Lark, 2004). Cassy regularly contributes projects to magazines such as *Jewelry Crafts*, *Step by Step Beads*, and *Polymer Café*. You can contact her at cassma@aol.com.

MICHELLE ROSS Michelle has been an artist and designer in various media all of her adult life. She began her working career as a potter, went on to graphic art, and worked in the film industry as a makeup artist for over twenty years. Michelle appeared as a regular guest on the *Carol Duvall Show* for fourteen seasons. She began designing jewelry in polymer clay and is currently passionate about Precious Metal Clay. *www.polymerclayplay.com*

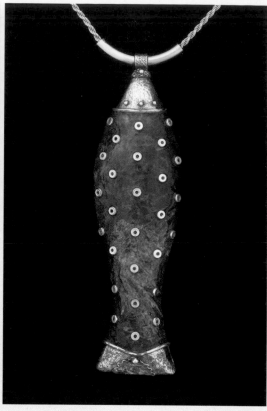

ABOVE: DESERT DREAMS *by Kelly Russell*
The center bead of this stunning necklace is made from textured PMC and PMC sheet, to which Kelly applied gold using the keum-boo technique. The focal point is a peacock feather protected by a sheet of mica. (Photo by Robert Diamante.)

ABOVE RIGHT: FISH PENDANT #3 *by Hattie Sanderson*
To add color to this pendant made from bisque-fired stoneware and PMC+, Hattie layered bits of torn paper towel that she dyed and painted. (Photo by Speedy Peacock.)

KELLY RUSSELL Kelly has worked in all sorts of art media, including watercolor, collage, intaglio printing, woodcuts, book-making, *katazome* (Japanese paste resist dyeing), found-object sculpture, beadwork, polymer clay, and silversmithing. She took a class in PMC about three years ago and has worked steadily with metal clay ever since, although she now likes to incorporate some of her other mediums into her pieces. *www.beadfuddled.com*

HATTIE SANDERSON Hattie Sanderson is an artist and instructor in the area of metal-smithing and metal clay. She is a PMC senior instructor and the creator of HattieS products and has produced metal clay instructional DVDs. Hattie's award-winning work has been exhibited internationally and published in several notable books and publications. *www.pmcsupply.com*

JACKIE TRUTY In April of 2000, Jackie, already a warm-glass and lapidary artist, first saw a demonstration on metal clay. She immediately knew she'd found her niche and soon became a senior instructor in Art Clay. In March of 2001, she accepted a position as one of two directors of education for Art Clay and later formed a partnership with Seigo Mukoyama and moved their newly acquired business, Art Clay World, USA, to Oak Lawn, Illinois. Now the sole administrator, Jackie runs the day-to-day operations as president, in addition to teaching and promoting Art Clay throughout North America. *www.artclayworld.com*

SHAHASP VALENTINE Shahasp began studying jewelry design at age thirteen. She continued her studies through high school and college and became the youngest fine jewelry manager in Macy's history. She later began creating jewelry professionally and started working with PMC in 1998. Shahasp's work falls into two distinct groups: a collection of historically inspired work and a series of organic designs inspired by nature. *www.precieux.com*

Suppliers

LISTED BELOW are the manufacturers and suppliers of many of the materials used in this book. Most of these companies sell their products to retail and online stores. Contact them directly to find a retailer near you.

ALLCRAFT
JEWELRY SUPPLY
800-645-7124
www.allcraftonline.com
Jewelrymaking tools and 24-karat-gold foil for keum-boo

AMACO®
800-374-1600
www.amaco.com
PolyBlade clay-cutting blades, polymer clay, tools, and cutters

ART CLAY
WORLD, USA
866-381-0100
www.artclayworld.com
Art Clay Silver products, metal clay supplies, and tools

THE ARTFUL
CRAFTER
877-321-2080
www.artfulcrafter.com
Mosaic tile supplies, tile nippers, metal clay, and beadmaking supplies

CLAY FACTORY, INC.
877-728-5739
www.clayfactoryinc.com
Polymer clay, tools, and general supplies

THE COMPLEAT
SCULPTOR, INC.
800-9-SCULPT
www.sculpt.com
Winterstone® Sculpting Stone and moldmaking and sculpting supplies

CREATIVE TEXTURE
TOOLS™
708-488-9589
www.creativetexturetools.com
Metal clay texture tools and keum-boo supplies

DELTA®
800-423-4135
www.deltacrafts.com
Sobo glue and Paint Jewels Glossy Colors

ENVIRONMENTAL
TECHNOLOGY, INC.
707-443-9323
www.eti-usa.com
Envirotex Lite and EasyCast epoxy resins

EARTHENWOOD
STUDIO
www.earthenwoodstudio.com
Ceramic faces, beads, and tiles

FIRE MOUNTAIN GEMS
800-355-2137
www.firemountaingems.com
Fine silver wire, findings, and stringing supplies

GOSS DESIGN STUDIO
www.makersgallery.com
Information on concrete for jewel-rymaking and book (Concrete Handbook for Artists)

HARBOR FREIGHT
TOOLS
800-444-3353
www.harborfreight.com
Hardware, tools, metal punches, and letter stamps

HEIDI GRACE DESIGNS
866-89-HEIDI
www.heidigrace.com
Glass Effects acrylic shapes

SHERRI HAAB
DESIGNS
www.sherrihaab.com
Books, workshops, craft kits, and Image Transfer Solution™

JACQUARD
PRODUCTS/RUPERT
GIBBON & SPIDER INC.
800-442-0455
www.jacquardproducts.com
Pearl Ex powdered pigments

JEC PRODUCTS
309-523-2600
www.jecproducts.com
Ultra-Lite Beehive Kiln, PMC products, tools, and accessories

KEMPER TOOLS
909-627-6191
www.kempertools.com
Klay Kutters and other sculpting tools and supplies

LACIS
510-843-7178
www.lacis.com
Ribbon, lace, buttons, and Kanagawa and Gudebrod brand silk cords

LAZERTRAN
800-245-7547
www.lazertran.com
*Lazertran Silk waterslide decal
transfer papers*

MICRO-SURFACE
FINISHING
PRODUCTS, INC.
800-225-3006
www.micro-surface.com
*Polishing tools and materials,
including Micro-Mesh®
cushioned abrasives, mesh
sheets, polishing swabs, and
liquid abrasives*

MOONDANCE
DESIGNS
www.moondancedesigns.com
*Beads and stringing materials,
jewelry findings, and C-Lon #18
nylon cord*

PIECEMAKERS
COUNTRY STORE
714-641-3112
www.piecemakers.com
*Craft supplies, polymer clay, and
Kanagawa silk cord*

PLAID
ENTERPRISES, INC.
800-842-4197
www.plaidonline.com
Mod Podge decoupage glue

PMC CONNECTION
866-PMC-CLAY
www.pmcconnection.com
*PMC products, tools, jewelry
findings, stones, and kilns*

PMC SUPPLY
800-388-2001
www.pmcsupply.com
*PMC clay, tools, starter
kits, DVDs, SpeedFire Cone,
Image Transfer Solution,
MultiMandrel™, HattieS products,
and fine silver casting grain*

POLYFORM PRODUCTS
www.sculpey.com
*Sculpey™ and Premo® polymer
clay products*

POLYMER CLAY EXPRESS
800-844-0138
www.polymerclayexpress.com
*Polymer clay, clay shapers,
blades, clay cutters, findings,
and tools*

PROVO CRAFT
800-937-7686
www.provocraft.com
Art Accentz Beedz

RIO GRANDE
800-545-6566
www.riogrande.com
*PMC products and supplies,
jewelry findings, kilns, torches,
silicon rubber putty, and
Colores epoxy resin*

SILVER CREEK
LEATHER CO.
812-945-8520
www.silvercreekleather.com
*Leather wristbands, hardware,
and supplies*

TANDY LEATHER
FACTORY
800-433-3201
www.tandyleather.com
*Leather, hardware, tools, and
supplies*

UGOTGLASS/GLASS
ORCHIDS
866-DICHRO-A
www.ugotglass.com
*Dichroic glass, metal clay,
findings, and supplies*

VOLCANO ARTS
209-296-6535
www.volcanoarts.biz
*Jewelrymaking supplies, rivets,
metal blocks, and anvils*

WHOLE LOTTA
WHIMSY
520-531-1966
www.wholelottawhimsy.com
*PMC, kilns, stones, metal clay,
and enameling supplies*

Other Jewelrymaking Books by Sherri Haab

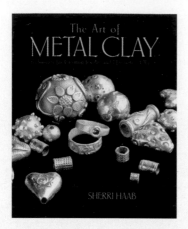

THE ART OF METAL CLAY

A comprehensive introduction to the medium—detailing the essentials of working, firing, and finishing—that also demonstrates how it can be textured, molded, carved, and sculpted to create beads, bracelets, pendants, earrings, rings, and other jewelry settings; boxes and vessels; and mixed media pieces that incorporate glass, epoxy resin, and polymer clay.

ISBN-10: 0-8230-0367-1
ISBN-13: 978-0-8230-0367-9

BEADED MACRAMÉ JEWELRY

A thorough introduction to macramé that includes an overview of essential materials and demonstrates basic knotting techniques. Fully illustrated projects show how to make bracelets, earrings, rings, and necklaces, plus a belt, a purse, and an iPod pouch, out of colorful, fine cords and shimmering beads.

ISBN-10: 0-8230-2952-2
ISBN-13: 978-0-8230-2952-5

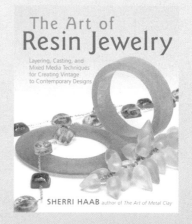

DESIGNER STYLE JEWELRY

Features the latest techniques for making stunning jewelry out of wire, beads, polymer clay, leather, resin, laminate, shrink plastic, and more, along with illustrated, step-by-step projects for earrings, necklaces, pendants, pins, bracelets, and rings.

ISBN-10: 0-8230-2601-9
ISBN-13: 978-0-8230-2601-2

THE ART OF RESIN JEWELRY

Shows how to use resin to create beautiful necklaces, bangles, bracelets, pins, earrings, and rings. Instructions include how to add colorants and other materials, how to cast three-dimensional forms, how to make your own molds, and how to combine resin with polymer clay.

ISBN-10: 0-8230-0344-2
ISBN-13: 978-0-8230-0344-0

Available from Watson-Guptill Publications
www.watsonguptill.com